Franklin & Marshall College

Lancaster, Pennsylvania

Written by Ellen Baier

Edited by Adam Burns and Jaime Myers

Layout by Meryl Sustarsic

*Additional contributions by Omid Gohari,
Christina Koshzow, Chris Mason, Joey Rahimi,
and Luke Skurman*

ISBN # 1-4274-0062-8
ISSN # 1551-0110
© Copyright 2006 College Prowler
All Rights Reserved
Printed in the U.S.A.
www.collegeprowler.com

Last Updated 5/16/06

Special Thanks To: Babs Carryer, Andy Hannah, LaunchCyte, Tim O'Brien, Bob Sehlinger, Thomas Emerson, Andrew Skurman, Barbara Skurman, Bert Mann, Dave Lehman, Daniel Fayock, Chris Babyak, The Donald H. Jones Center for Entrepreneurship, Terry Slease, Jerry McGinnis, Bill Ecenberger, Idie McGinty, Kyle Russell, Jacque Zaremba, Larry Winderbaum, Roland Allen, Jon Reider, Team Evankovich, Lauren Varacalli, Abu Noaman, Mark Exler, Daniel Steinmeyer, Jared Cohon, Gabriela Oates, David Koegler, and Glen Meakem.

Bounce-Back Team: Sara Sprunk, Katie Oppenheimer, and Austin D. Williams.

College Prowler®
5001 Baum Blvd.
Suite 750
Pittsburgh, PA 15213

Phone: 1-800-290-2682
Fax: 1-800-772-4972
E-Mail: info@collegeprowler.com
Web Site: www.collegeprowler.com

Welcome to College Prowler®

During the writing of College Prowler's guidebooks, we felt it was critical that our content was unbiased and unaffiliated with any college or university. We think it's important that our readers get honest information and a realistic impression of the student opinions on any campus—that's why if any aspect of a particular school is terrible, we (unlike a campus brochure) intend to publish it. While we do keep an eye out for the occasional extremist—the cheerleader or the cynic—we take pride in letting the students tell it like it is. We strive to create a book that's as representative as possible of each particular campus. Our books cover both the good and the bad, and whether the survey responses point to recurring trends or a variation in opinion, these sentiments are directly and proportionally expressed through our guides.

College Prowler guidebooks are in the hands of students throughout the entire process of their creation. Because you can't make student-written guides without the students, we have students at each campus who help write, randomly survey their peers, edit, layout, and perform accuracy checks on every book that we publish. From the very beginning, student writers gather the most up-to-date stats, facts, and inside information on their colleges. They fill each section with student quotes and summarize the findings in editorial reviews. In addition, each school receives a collection of letter grades (A through F) that reflect student opinion and help to represent contentment, prominence, or satisfaction for each of our 20 specific categories. Just as in grade school, the higher the mark the more content, more prominent, or more satisfied the students are with the particular category.

Once a book is written, additional students serve as editors and check for accuracy even more extensively. Our bounce-back team—a group of randomly selected students who have no involvement with the project—are asked to read over the material in order to help ensure that the book accurately expresses every aspect of the university and its students. This same process is applied to the 200-plus schools College Prowler currently covers. Each book is the result of endless student contributions, hundreds of pages of research and writing, and countless hours of hard work. All of this has led to the creation of a student information network that stretches across the nation to every school that we cover. It's no easy accomplishment, but it's the reason that our guides are such a great resource.

When reading our books and looking at our grades, keep in mind that every college is different and that the students who make up each school are not uniform—as a result, it is important to assess schools on a case-by-case basis. Because it's impossible to summarize an entire school with a single number or description, each book provides a dialogue, not a decision, that's made up of 20 different topics and hundreds of student quotes. In the end, we hope that this guide will serve as a valuable tool in your college selection process. Enjoy!

OMID GOHARI ○ CHRISTINA KOSHZOW ○ CHRIS MASON ○ JOEY RAHIMI ○ LUKE SKURMAN ○
The College Prowler Team

Table of Contents

Introduction from the Author

A school search is typically a source of anxiety, as the eager high-school student tries to reconcile both a dizzying amount of statistics and the unquantifiable feelings each campus triggers. I remember a particular trip I took with my parents: six schools in seven days! I loved three of them, liked two, and categorically refused to set foot on the sixth after only a glance. Who knows why some campuses strike us the way they do? It is my hope that this guide will inform you as you try to make your choice. Although campus visits are wonderful, they're only a day or two, so it is impossible to really get at the heart of a school.

The essence of Franklin & Marshall College is that its students care about their studies, but more importantly, they care about the citizens that they will become. Caring, involved, and enthusiastic, F&M students spend their four (or three and a half to five) years in Lancaster, on that 170-acre piece of paradise in the middle of a city, learning how to teach themselves, once they graduate, by the example set by their professors. The students are valued members of a community, prized for their knowledge and hard work, and they're given almost infinite scope for their drive, enthusiasm, and determination to succeed. But their ambition doesn't have the hypercompetitive drive of an MIT or University of Chicago. Instead, F&M students come to themselves amidst a welcoming, vibrant community of peers, both fellow students and faculty. Students do research, both original and as contributors to larger studies, perform experiments, put on shows, and learn to think, write, and create.

It is my hope that you, in your college search, will come to admire and love F&M as much as I do now. I want to be honest as you learn about F&M—no school is perfect, and Franklin & Marshall is no exception to the rule. F&M students do complain, but we do so perfectly content in the knowledge that our concerns will be heard, recognized, and addressed. Our president's door is never closed to us, administrators know hundreds of us by name and most of us by face, and of course, e-mail is 24/7. Everyone, from the greenest first-year to the most blasé senior, makes a difference in the quality of life at F&M.

Ellen Baier, Author
Franklin & Marshall College

By the Numbers

General Information

Franklin & Marshall College
P.O. Box 3003
Lancaster, PA 17604

Control:
Private

Academic Calendar:
Semester

Religious Affiliation:
None

Founded:
1787

Web Site:
www.fandm.edu

Main Phone:
(717) 291-3911

Admissions Phone:
(717) 291-3953

Student Body

**Full-Time
Undergraduates:**
1,933

**Part-Time
Undergraduates:**
39

**Total Male
Undergraduates:**
1,052

**Total Female
Undergraduates:**
920

Admissions

Overall Acceptance Rate:
49%

Early Decision Acceptance Rate:
72%

Regular Acceptance Rate:
47%

Total Applicants:
4,070

Total Acceptances:
2,010

Total Freshman Enrollment:
31

Yield (% of admitted students who actually enroll):
26%

Early Decision Available?
Yes

Early Action Available?
No

Early Decision One Deadline:
November 15

Early Decision Two Deadline:
January 15

Early Decision One Notification:
December 15

Early Decision Two Notification:
February 15

Regular Decision Deadline:
February 1

Regular Decision Notification:
April 1

Must-Reply-By Date:
May 1

Applicants Placed on Waiting List:
982

Applicants Accepted from Waiting List:
2,010

Students Enrolled from Waiting List:
76

Transfer Applications Received:
69

Transfer Applications Accepted:
37

Transfer Students Enrolled:
24

Transfer Application Acceptance Rate:
53%

Common Application Accepted?
Yes

Supplemental Forms Required?
Yes

Admissions E-Mail:
admission@fandm.edu

Admissions Web Site:
http://admission.fandm.edu

SAT I or ACT Required?
Either

**SAT I Range
(25th–75th Percentile):**
1170–1360

**SAT I Verbal Range
(25th–75th Percentile):**
580–670

**SAT I Math Range
(25th–75th Percentile):**
590–690

Retention Rate:
90%

**Top 10% of High
School Class:**
49%

Application Fee:
$50

Financial Information

Tuition:
$32,530

Room and Board:
$8,060

Books and Supplies:
$650

**Average Need-Based
Financial Aid Package
(including loans, work-study,
grants, and other sources):**
$23,456

**Students Who Applied for
Financial Aid:**
75%

Students Who Recieved Aid:
40%

Financial Aid Forms Deadline:
February 1

Financial Aid Phone:
(717) 291-3991

Financial Aid E-Mail:
financialaid@fandm.edu

Financial Aid Web Site:
*www.fandm.edu/financial
aid.xml*

Academics

The Lowdown On...
Academics

Degree Awarded:
Bachelor

Most Popular Majors:
20% Political Science and
　　Government
10% Accounting and Finance
10% Business Administration
　　and Management
　8% English
　8% Psychology

Full-time Faculty:
161

**Faculty with
Terminal Degree:**
96%

**Student-to-Faculty
Ratio:**
11:1

Average Course Load:

4 classes per semester
(equivalent to 16 credit hours)

Graduation Rates:

Four-Year: 78%
Five-Year: 82%
Six-Year: 82%

Special Degree Options

Joint Major – Complete the requirements of a major from two departments

Special Studies Major – With your advisor, design your own major from among three or more departments

Education – Cooperative program with local Millersville University

Engineering – 3/2 and 4/2 programs with Penn State, Case Western Reserve, Columbia, Washington University in St. Louis, and Rensselaer Polytechnic Institute

Forestry and environmental studies – 3/2 or 4/2 program with Duke University

AP Test Score Requirements

Credit for scores of 4 or 5; Language Studies requirement is met by a score of 3 or higher

IB Test Score Requirements

Credit for scores of 5 or higher for each higher level examination taken; 8 course credits (1 full year) will be granted to IB degree recipients with a total score of 30 or higher

Sample Academic Clubs

Black Pyramid, Chess Club, Circolo Italiano, Economics Club, History Club, Physics and Astronomy Club, Porter Scientific Society, Prolog, Skull and Cross Society

Best Places to Study

Shadek-Fackenthal Library, Martin Science Library, Keiper Lounge (3rd floor)

Affiliated Study Abroad Programs

Advanced Studies in England

One- or two-semester programs in British studies stressing literature, history, art history, and women's studies from the Middle Ages through the twentieth century. ASE also offers a five-week summer session focusing on British studies.

American School of Classical Studies in Athens

Six-week summer sessions on Greek history, literature, and culture, with field trips to sites and museums in and beyond Attica.

Denmark's International Study Program

One- or two-semester programs, including humanities and social sciences, international business, architecture and design, and marine biology and ecology. Most participants live with Danish families. Danish language instruction is optional.

Institute for the International Education of Students

One- or two-semester and summer programs in Europe, Asia, Latin America, and Australia. In most locations, students with sufficient knowledge of the language take courses directly in a foreign university.

Intercollegiate Center for Classical Studies in Rome

One- or two-semester programs in Greek and Latin literature, history, art, archeology, supplemented by field trips within Italy.

The Swedish Program

One- or two-semester program sponsored by Stockholm University and a consortium of American colleges and universities. Located in the capital city of Stockholm, the program provides students with an opportunity to study, in English, how Sweden has addressed political, social, artistic, and economic issues relevant to all advanced societies. Topics are pursued in an interdisciplinary and critical tradition. Students study film, literature, history, languages, philosophy, psychology, and biology.

A number of other programs are available, and many F&M students enjoy their sophomore or junior year abroad.

Did You Know?

 F&M began life as two colleges: Franklin College began with an **endowment from Benjamin Franklin**, and Marshall College, founded in Mercersburg by first Supreme Court Chief Justice John Marshall. In 1853, the two colleges merged, because Franklin College had no money and Marshall College had no students.

Franklin College was the first bilingual college in the United States **using English and German**.

Franklin College was **founded in a brewery**.

Franklin & Marshall is the **25th oldest college** in the U.S.

Franklin & Marshall went co-educational in 1969, when the first class with women was admitted.

F&M doesn't use teaching assistants. The closest thing available are preceptors, who are upperclassmen "advisors" to a Foundation course or a First-Year Seminar. The preceptors hold extra discussion sessions or offer to help write papers.

F&M's Foundations requirement is a unique system of inter-subjective courses taught by faculty in each department, which are divided into three basic groups: **Community, Culture, and Society; the Natural World; and Mind, Self, and Spirit**. Students must take one course from each group during their first four semesters. This system allows a wide exposure to a number of disciplines; it is ideal for a student who is unsure of his or her major.

About 90 percent of F&M students who applied to medical schools were **accepted by at least one school**; the national acceptance rate is about half of that.

Close to 90 percent of F&M seniors who apply to law school get accepted.

Academics

> "My teachers have been inspiring. They have enriched my life. Classes have been interesting for the most part, especially when teachers abandon the traditional lecture format and engage us in dialogue, discussion, and use multimedia."

Q "I was fortunate enough to have amazing professors my freshman year—engaging, enthusiastic, personable. They made **a concentrated effort to draw their students into the subject at hand**. But beware, the boring ones are out there! If you're really worried about professors, or classes for that matter, come do an Overnight and take a class that sounds interesting to you. Decide/find out for yourself! (Or, you can trust me, as I'm quite reliable.) As for the classes, I try to take what I'm interested in, so I usually find them interesting (naturally). Why suffer through honors calculus if your passion is the current lifestyles of aboriginal Australians, or vice versa?"

Q "The professors are generally **rather passionate about their pursuits** and definitely take the time to talk to students, get people engaged, and make plenty of time for office hours and appointments. I have had several profs who took an active interest in me beyond my grades, and we have become good friends."

Q "For the most part, the teachers are amazing. They are interested in their students and absolutely love the subjects they are teaching. They are **extremely devoted to what they do**. I've only taken a couple of classes that didn't interest me, and that had very little to do with the professors and a lot to do with me figuring out what I wanted to study."

Q "Teachers are **well prepared, friendly, and always willing to help you understand** a concept. I find most of my classes interesting. Foundations, not so much, but I've liked my science and language classes."

Q "I have found some classes at F&M very interesting. I have loved all of the government classes I took. The teachers were interesting, and also interested in what the students had to say. They **always encourage discussion, and also debate**, which is what really made the classes interesting."

Q "I have also loved the Jewish history classes I took. Professor D. was by far my favorite professor at F&M, and I'm sad that he left to teach at a different school. He was a **really good-hearted teacher** who actually really knew the subjects that he was teaching. He was really knowledgeable in Jewish history, which made the class enjoyable because his lectures just seemed to flow well."

Q "As for professors that teach courses for my [Spanish] major, I haven't really enjoyed any of them very much. I find that **some of the Spanish teachers tend to be either misleading or even condescending**, but despite my dislike for the professors I did enjoy most of the Spanish classes I have taken thus far. The literature we read is actually quite good."

Q "I think most of the teachers here make an effort in getting to know you. They are super-busy, but **they always have time for their students**."

Q "I am constantly impressed with the faculty here. I think when a lot of people apply to college, they look for professors at the forefront of their field, but forget to find out whether or not they're good teachers. I have always had professors here who not only are **intelligent, creative, and interesting**, but they actually engage the class instead of standing and lecturing for an hour and a half. The faculty also takes an active interest in you as a student here at F&M. Most of my profs know my name before I know theirs! And, they always take the time to talk with you even when their concern, or yours, isn't necessarily an academic one."

The College Prowler Take On...
Academics

Although all teaching styles may not appeal to all students, most students feel that the quality of education they're receiving at F&M is very high. They enjoy their classes and appreciate teachers with creative and innovative approaches to the classroom, as well as friendly attitudes toward students outside of the classroom.

Academics are top-notch here at F&M, with steep admission requirements and devoted faculty at the top of their fields. The reputation of the sciences at F&M is stellar at medical schools. Franklin & Marshall-trained chemists, and geoscientists in particular, are in high demand at graduate schools across the country, as are our social scientists in disciplines such as anthropology, economics, and sociology.

B+

The College Prowler® Grade on

Academics: B+

A high Academics grade generally indicates that professors are knowledgeable, accessible, and genuinely interested in their students' welfare. Other determining factors include class size, how well professors communicate, and whether or not classes are engaging.

Local Atmosphere

The Lowdown On...
Local Atmosphere

Region:
Midatlantic

City, State:
Lancaster, PA

Setting:
Small city

Distance from Philadelphia:
1 hour, 20 minutes

Distance from Baltimore:
1 hour, 15 minutes

Distance from NYC:
2 hours, 45 minutes

Distance from DC:
2 hours

→

Points of Interest:

Fulton Opera House
12 N. Prince St.
Lancaster
(717) 394-7133

Heritage Center Museum
13 W. King St.
Penn Square
(717) 299-6440

Hershey Park
100 W. Hersheypark Dr.
Hershey, PA 17033
(800) HERSHEY

James Buchanan's Wheatland
1120 Marietta Ave.
Lancaster
(717) 392-8721

PA Renaissance Faire
Route 72 N.
Manheim
(717) 665-7021

Rainbow Dinner Theatre
3065 Lincoln Highway E.
Paradise
(800) 292-4301

Watch & Clock Museum
514 Poplar St.
Columbia
(717) 684-8261

Closest Shopping Malls or Plazas:

King of Prussia Mall
Park City Center
York Galleria

Closest Movie Theater:

Regal Manor 16 Cinemas
1246 Millersville Pke.
Lancaster
(717) 392-1511

Major Sports Teams:

Baltimore Orioles (baseball)
Baltimore Ravens (football)
Harrisburg Senators
(AA baseball)
Philadelphia 76ers
(basketball)
Philadelphia Eagles (football)
Philadelphia Flyers (hockey)
Philadelphia Phillies
(baseball)
New Jersey Devils (hockey)
New Jersey Nets (basketball)

Did You Know?

5 Fun Facts about Lancaster:

- **Free wine** every month at First Friday downtown!
- Bird-in-Hand, Blue Ball, Intercourse, and Virginville **are all towns** in Lancaster County.
- The **movie *Witness* was filmed here**, and many locals were extras.
- The Central Market is one of **the oldest farmer's markets** in the country.
- Cow-tipping is considered **a perfectly valid sport**.

Famous People from Lancaster:

James Buchanan – Fifteenth president of the U.S.

Benjamin Rush – Early surgeon and physician

Andrew Wyeth – Artist

Local Slang:

Lancaster is in the heart of Pennsylvania Dutch country; all of these expressions are heavily influenced by the version of German that the local Amish and Mennonites currently speak, though these words are not limited to the Plain Folk.

All – Empty. "This can is all! Get me another, please."

Awhile – While you wait, a waitress might say, "Can I bring you a Coke awhile?"

Coke – Any fizzy beverage. "What kind of Coke do you want?"

Dassent – Dare not. "I want to break the rules, but I see a cop, so I dassent."

English – A non-Amish person, whatever his or her actual nationality is.

Fasnacht – Dough fried in fat. The day before Ash Wednesday is known as Fasnacht Day in Lancaster County, and fasnacht is served in the dining hall.

Het up – Emotional, shaken up, riled. "I was about to start a fight, I was so het up!"

Mind on – Recall. "Do you mind on that nice college boy who used to come by here?"

Outen the lights – Turn off the lights. "Would you outen the lights when you leave, please?"

Plain Folk – The Amish, who shun electricity and other modern conveniences. You can frequently see their horse-drawn buggies around Lancaster County.

Redd up – Tidy up, clean; put a room in order. "Monday is redd-up day, so get your things in order."

Wants on – To like somebody and want to hook-up with them. "He's looking at me; I bet he wants on."

City Web Sites

www.co.lancaster.pa.us

www.cityoflancasterpa.com

www.lancasteronline.com

www.lancasterpa.net

Students Speak Out On...
Local Atmosphere

"Lancaster is actually a really cool place despite what a lot of people say. I have recently met some wonderful non-F&M people that I definitely don't want to lose touch with."

Q "I love the atmosphere of Lancaster. **It's a warm-hearted small town.** There are no other schools that I have interacted with, but Millersville is close by. In Lancaster, we explore art galleries every First Friday, see shows, shop, enjoy the outlets, tour the Amish farms, go bowling, and laser bowling. I have never been left with nothing to do!"

Q "Lancaster, for me, is a nice change of pace. It's a city in the middle of the country, so both ways of life are represented in an oddball conglomeration of shopping centers, traffic, fresh produce, and Mennonite buggies. Visitations required: Central Market and Angry, Young, and Poor (for those who enjoy LPs and punk rock). **Take the time to walk around downtown and discover things for yourself.** Millersville University is a hop away from us, as is Elizabethtown, although Millersville students are more present around Lancaster."

Q "There is a large state university, Millersville, in the next town. Generally, **Lancaster is kind of boring and segregated.** There isn't really a social life to be found off campus, which is why a lot of people seem to drink as their main extracurricular."

Q "Students generally stay on campus and keep within the F&M bubble, although **there are other colleges in the area**. Also, since a lot of upperclassmen live off campus, student/community relations aren't so good. The farmer's market is a fun place to visit with good food, too."

Q "I generally like the atmosphere of the town we are in. It's welcoming and comfortable. There aren't really any other universities around unless, you count the theology school across the street. I would have to say for stuff to visit would definitely be the outlets down Route 30 and also downtown Lancaster. There are **some great little coffee places** and art galleries there, and also a fantastic paint-your-own pottery place that I love going to! Also, every first Friday of the month is First Friday, where all the art galleries open and have free wine and snacks, so you can wander around and look at pretty artwork and get tipsy. It's good fun. Stuff to stay away from? Not so sure on that one . . . probably just the not so nice parts of town."

Q "Freshman year **there is so much to do on campus**, you almost forget that there's an entire city to explore. I've been wandering into town on 'adventures' and I have fallen in love with the city. With five schools in the area counting us (Millersville, E-town, the Lancaster School of Art, Steven's Technical College, F&M), there are a lot of young people around. And as for things to do, we have a lot, including theater, concerts in the park or at the Chameleon, coffee shops, restaurants, Central Market, the North Museum, art galleries, and some stuff I haven't even gotten around to finding yet."

Q "I don't really like Lancaster because I don't feel that the school and the community are close. I think that some of the **Lancaster residents consider us rich, spoiled kids** and don't give us much of a chance."

The College Prowler Take On...
Local Atmosphere

When Fummers are so inclined, they have a variety of events and cultural activities to attend. Lancaster is no New York City in terms of its theater, but the local downtown theater, Fulton Opera House, is nationally known to be of extremely high caliber. Cultural life has its lulls, though. The month of January, for example, might as well not exist. However, Lancaster is bigger than it feels, and it is not easy to exhaust the local entertainment options we have.

There's plenty for students to do around town, but local college-town relations have traditionally been strained. The James Street Improvement District is busily building relationships and helping students and "townies" get along better. But there are a few more fences to be mended.

The College Prowler® Grade on

Local Atmosphere: C-

A high Local Atmosphere grade indicates that the area surrounding campus is safe and scenic. Other factors include nearby attractions, proximity to other schools, and the town's attitude toward students.

Safety & Security

The Lowdown On...
Safety & Security

Number of F&M Police Officers:
23

Safety & Security Phone:
(717) 291-3939

Safety Services:
Emergency phones
Escort services
Rape Aggression Defense (RAD) classes

Health Center:
Appel Infirmary
(717) 291-4082
Hours: Monday–Friday 7:30 a.m.–5:30 p.m., Saturday 10 a.m.–12 p.m.

Health Services:
Basic health care
Referrals to counseling services
On-site pharmaceuticals
STD screening

Did You Know?

After-hours **medical care is available** at the Lancaster Regional Hospital emergency room, only two blocks from campus.

The **Department of Public Safety provides safety checks** to off-campus apartments during breaks upon request.

Students Speak Out On...
Safety & Security

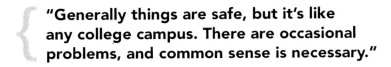

{ **"Generally things are safe, but it's like any college campus. There are occasional problems, and common sense is necessary."**

Q "I have always felt that the **college has done everything in its power to keep us safe**. There was a burglary next door [to me], and security was there very soon. I interact with F&M security all the time. When there are car break-ins or suspicious people, I never hesitate to call, and they always take me seriously. At night, walking home from the library, I can always see F&M security."

Q "Safety and security . . . well, they try hard. **Mostly they ride around on their bikes** and let kids in their rooms if they've been locked out. However, to be fair, I feel a lot safer if I'm walking home late at night/early morning, and I see them posted around campus."

Q "I have never felt unsafe at F&M; I feel that **the public safety people do a pretty good job**."

Q "The campus is basically a safe place, and **security does a sufficient job** in dealing with most reported problems."

Q "It's been **much better recently**. Most students whine about the security presence, but they're here to keep us safe."

Q "Security is much better. They have tried to install new lights and call boxes, so it seems like **they are making an effort** in making us feel safer on campus. The staff is also a lot friendlier than what it used to be. President Fry really turned things around."

Q "Security and safety on campus is quite good, I think. It has improved a lot over the years, or so I am told. But when I'm on campus and have to walk from building to building alone at night, I feel safe. You **always see security walking around campus**, or even riding bikes down the nearby streets that some students live on. Plus, the campus security car is constantly circling the roads around campus. So overall, I feel pretty safe. I've never personally had a problem, and hope that it stays that way."

Q "Safety and security are really great people. By now, most of them know me by name, **I call for an escort home when I'm out visiting friends** off campus. Safety and security has tripled in size since President Fry's arrival, and I've never felt unsafe."

The College Prowler Take On...
Safety & Security

Over the past couple years, the Department of Public Safety has more than doubled, which has helped the F&M community. The officers receive more mixed reviews, but their role is growing in campus life. F&M is near a not so good neighborhood where muggings have been known to occur, although the rise of public safety officers has dramatically curtailed this risk.

Appel (pronounced like the fruit) Infirmary's most frequent complaint is their lack of evening or weekend hours, which tends to be when students need emergency care most often. However, the local hospital, Lancaster Regional, is within walking distance, and many students have gone there when necessary. Appel maintains a 24-hour Rape Crisis Hotline and close ties to Counseling Services.

The College Prowler® Grade on
Safety & Security: B+

A high grade in Safety & Security means that students generally feel safe, campus police are visible, blue-light phones and escort services are readily available, and safety precautions are not overly necessary.

Computers

The Lowdown On...
Computers

High-Speed Network?

Yes

Wireless Network?

Yes, in places such as the Hartman Green, the Quad, the fitness center, all housing, classrooms, and the stacks in the libraries

Number of Computers:

272

Operating Systems:

Mac, OS X

24-Hour Labs:

None

Number of Labs:

5 for use by all students, as well as several for the use of specific departments or majors

Free Software

Programs such as Adobe Acrobat Reader, Microsoft Office, Microsoft Explorer, Safari, Eudora, SPSS, Mathematica, and Virex are all free.

Discounted Software

Not necessary. Most software needed for class can be found on the software server.

Charge to Print?

In high traffic labs, printing costs are two and a half cents per page to print on both sides of the paper and five cents per page to print on only one side. There are some smaller labs that have no charge to print, which are scattered over the campus.

Did You Know?

F&M was one of the most unwired campuses in the States, according to the Intel Corporation "**Most Unwired College Campuses**" survey that ranks the top 100 schools for wireless computing access.

F&M boasts "smart" **classrooms that are fully wired** for network access, as well as several mobile "classrooms," consisting of a cart with wireless laptops.

MyDiplomat, an intranet informational system, offers full **access to personalized data** for all members of the campus community.

Students Speak Out On...
Computers

"I would recommend having your own computer because the labs tend to be the most crowded at the absolute most inconvenient times. Plus, it's just nice to be able to work in your own room."

Q "The computer labs are **crowded during certain times of the day (night)**, and during finals, but it's generally not a problem getting on a computer. I have my own computer, which I would recommend just for convenience's sake (e-mail, IM, working when the libraries are closed)."

Q "The computer network is nice and zippy, unless it's down, which happens occasionally, although not enough to slow anyone's essay progress or research. As for the labs, this is what I've found: Shad-Fack's (the main library) is nice, quiet, empty most of the time. If you're trying to get in there during mid-terms or finals, however, forget it. Bring a pillow and camp out, or you're not getting a computer. I don't really like Martin's (the science library) computer labs, mostly because **everyone talks constantly, and it's hard to get work done**. Definitely have your own computer! It's practically a must on this campus. We are a Mac school, so they're preferred, but I have friends who get along fine with their PCs. Having a Mac just makes your life a little bit easier, plus they can do a lot of nifty things PCs can't. (Do I get paid for this free advertising?)"

Q "**It would make your life easier to have a computer**. During peak hours of 10 a.m. to midnight, the labs can get crowded. During exam week, it is very hard to find one. I have been very pleased with computing and the speed of the network."

Q "It would be best to have your own computer; however, I often work in the computer workroom in the science library. However, **it tends to be noisy at night** as the students gather to study and finish papers."

Q "The computer network is great. **It's fast, easy, and convenient**. The computer labs are generally not that crowded. They only get crowded around midterms and finals, otherwise, you can almost always find a computer to use. I would still bring my own computer because, personally it's just easier that way. It's nice to be able to have a computer to use whenever I want and also for whatever I want."

Q "The computer network is nice. **You can always find an open computer in the library**, but I would bring your own just because you will end up using it so much."

Q "I received a computer with my scholarship and **the tech support has been great**!"

The College Prowler Take On...
Computers

If you want a life, you'll have a computer. AOL Instant Messenger is the only way students communicate anymore, and they do it constantly. F&M is a fully Mac campus, and the computer store offers freshmen laptops at a decent markdown. Over 90 percent of Franklin & Marshall students own their own computers. The lucky students who are recipients of the Marshall Scholarship receive their computers for free, as do Rauch Scholars. However, PC owners are out of luck, because no Windows machines are sold or supported by the campus.

The wireless network on campus is fairly decent with strong signals in the most popular gathering places. However, the school does have some file-sharing safeguards in place, so programs like Limewire, Kazaa, and Acquisition are advised against in practical terms, if not moral ones. If you don't have a computer, both Martin Science Library and Shadek-Fackenthal Library have labs and computer classrooms. Martin's is open until 2 a.m., and Shaddy's until midnight (except on Friday and Saturday nights, when they each close two hours earlier). They're frequently crowded. During midterm and finals time, you should probably hire thugs to help you get a spot.

The College Prowler® Grade on

Computers: B

A high grade in Computers designates that computer labs are available, the computer network is easily accessible, and the campus' computing technology is up-to-date.

Facilities

The Lowdown On...
Facilities

Student Center:
Steinman College Center
(containing the Atrium)

Libraries:
Shadek-Fackenthal

Martin Science

Psychology
(in Whitely Building)

Academic Technology
Services (in the basement
of Stager Hall)

Campus Size:
170 acres

Popular Places to Chill:
Ben's Underground

Jazzman's Café

Steinman College Center/
Common Ground

What Is There to Do on Campus?

A fan of jazz and blues? Join the Bessie Smith Society at their weekly shows. Into theater and music? Check out shows at Roschel, classical concerts at Barshinger, and special events at the Green Room. Rather just rent a movie? Spectacles, the on-campus video store, has a great selection and $1 rentals. There's always Ben's Underground where you can shoot some pool or play foosball. And of course, hanging out at the Atrium with a bunch of friends is a great option. There are also choral groups, three a cappella groups, bands, and orchestras for the more musically inclined to join.

Movie Theater on Campus?

On most Fridays and Saturdays, popular movies enjoy a second run in Barshinger Hall for only $1 ($3 for non-students). Campus Entertainment Committee (CEC) accepts movie requests for the following semester.

Bowling on Campus?

No

Bar on Campus?

No

Coffeehouse on Campus?

Ben's Underground offers a "coffeehouse series" with live music and other events. Also, Jazzman's Café in Distler Bookstore and Pandini's in the Steinman College Center are both specialty coffee bars.

Favorite Things to Do on Campus

The Spring Arts Festival is a huge student favorite. For a weekend in April, dozens of bands are invited to play on the Green and Quad, student artwork is displayed, and cultural events proliferate, as does drinking! Of-age students are permitted to drink, and under-age students aren't exactly discouraged. You couldn't do everything if you stayed for eight Spring Arts Weekends. And of course, you can't ever have too much of a good thing, and people are agitating for a Fall Arts Weekend! This is besides the huge concert each semeste. Past bands have included LIVE, Rusted Root, and Dispatch.

For more day-to-day excitement, students stir up debates in the weekly *College Reporter* and bimonthly *College Dispatch*, or work on the award-winning yearbook, the *Oriflamme*. Dancers have plenty of scope with the Dance Club, Dance Team, Ballroom Dancing Club, and a number of courses and master classes each semester. Want a radio show? The F&M radio station is award-winning as well and can be heard in many students' rooms, as well as in the dining hall.

Athletic Centers

The Alumni Sports and Fitness Center (ASFC) is a state-of-the-art fitness center with Olympic-sized pool, exercise room, and suspended track. Mayser Gym is home to the varisty basketball gym, and has and four squash courts, team locker rooms, and a training room. The Strength Training Center (The Pit) is a free weight room in the facilities and operations building behind Thomas Hall.

Students Speak Out On...
Facilities

"The athletic facilities, which includes the workout center is great; there are tons of ellipticals, and the facilities are excellent. There is a newer student union bookstore and coffeehouse and possible renovations to other student spaces."

Q "**The facilities are nice and updated**; I have no complaints."

Q "The facilities are, **for the most part, pretty nice**. A little updating wouldn't hurt, but they all suffice."

Q "The athletics facilities are quite nice. There is a nice big pool, nice big track (suspended, gasp!), nice big basketball courts, and a nice big exercise room. Our student center is pretty nice, but it's still old and in need of much overhauling. I feel **they're making a concentrated effort** to get all of our facilities up to excellent quality, not just the sports facilities, as it was last year."

Q "The ASFC (Alumni Sports and Fitness Center) and computer workrooms are kept orderly and clean. The student center is also **a big hangout for most students**, and it's comfortable."

Q "On-campus facilities are **far superior to campuses of comparable size**."

Q "The athletic center across the street is great! I am a frequent visitor. They keep all the gym equipment **clean and also up to date**. They just bought a bunch of new machines this past year. The computer centers are pretty good, too. They're quiet if you're the type of person who needs silence while doing work. The student center is all right. It's always packed around lunchtime, especially the Common Ground, so it'd be great if there was some more space and more chairs. It'd also be great if the mailroom had more hours. I mean, three hours in the morning on Saturday is awful. No one is even awake until after noon."

Q "I love the campus facilities. I think **the school does a great job maintaining all of our buildings**, and other than not being open late enough for my tastes, they do a great job."

Q "If you're into the arts, you're in luck! **We've built a gorgeous theater**, the Roschel Center for the Performing Arts. This is on top of the Barshinger Hall and puts musicians, singers, dancers, and actors in seventh heaven. It's too bad, of course, that they didn't allot funds to staff the new building; the Department of Theater, Dance, and Film stretched its staff's resources to the limit to run the Center in its first year."

Q "These two performance centers have been built to help strengthen the arts at **a very science-focused school**. The chemistry, biology, and geology departments have typically been the most popular and most heavily-funded departments on campus, with excellent resources."

Q "The Writers' House, a space for poets and writers was built, and a Barnes and Nobles bookstore is in the center of campus. **Construction has been heavy on campus**, and the administration is tirelessly looking for new ways to improve the campus. Look forward to many new, lovely buildings and facilities."

The College Prowler Take On...
Facilities

A number of new student buildings have popped up over the last decade, and students love the new spaces. President John Fry always has a capital campaign going on to raise funds for a new building, and now is no exception. Currently in the works is a $40 million Life Sciences building, intended to house the psychology, biology, and philosophy departments, as well as several interdisciplinary programs. It is expected to be open for the Fall of 2007. Expect to see construction nearly constantly, but then again, that means that students will have new buildings pop up around them each year.

Several new buildings are great resources for students. The Barnes and Noble bookstore inside the renovated Distler House includes a coffee shop. The Writers' House, a two-story building with the feel of a home is ample space for Writing Center tutors, a reading room, performance space, and two seminar rooms. And of course, the gorgeous Roschel Performing Arts Center. The school is devoted to the creation of new public areas with 98 new, high-efficiency laundry machines. However, students keep asking for later hours, as very little is open late except the Steinman Center is open until 2 a.m.

The College Prowler® Grade on

Facilities: A-

A high Facilities grade indicates that the campus is aesthetically pleasing and well-maintained; facilities are state-of-the-art, and libraries are exceptional. Other determining factors include the quality of both athletic and student centers and an abundance of things to do on campus.

Campus Dining

The Lowdown On...
Campus Dining

Freshman Meal Plan Requirement?

Yes, 225 block meals, including five guest meals and $120 in Flex dollars (used only at the Common Ground, for retail items such as bottled soda, or for extras over the meal plan allotment)

Meal Plan Average Cost:

$2,810 per year

Places to Grab a Bite with Your Meal Plan:

Jazzman's Café

Location: Distler

Food: Specialty coffees, pastries

Hours: Monday-Thursday 7:30 a.m.–12 a.m., Friday 7:30 a.m.–6 p.m., Saturday 11 a.m.–5 p.m., Sunday 11 a.m. –12 a.m.

The Marketplace

Location: Between North and South Ben Franklin dorms

Food: Buffet-style Mexican, American deli, Italian

Hours: Monday–Saturday
7:30 a.m.–10:30 a.m.,
11 a.m.–1:30 p.m.,
5 p.m.–7:45 p.m.,
Sunday 11 a.m.–1:30 p.m.,
5 p.m.–7:45 p.m.

Pandini's

Location: Steinman College Center

Food: Pizza, pasta, salads, coffee

Hours: Monday–Friday
8 a.m.–1:30 a.m., Saturday
6 p.m. –1:30 a.m.

Quizno's

Location: Marshall-Buchanan patio

Food: Toasted subs

Hours: Monday–Friday
12 p.m.–1 a.m., Saturday–Sunday 2 p.m.–1 a.m.

Salsa Rico and Sky Ranch Grill

Location: Ben Franklin

Hours: Monday–Friday
11 a.m.–9 p.m.,
Sunday 5 p.m.–9 p.m.

24-Hour On-Campus Eating?

No

Student Favorites:

Pandini's

Off-Campus Places to Use Your Meal Plan:

None, but College Corner Café will accept Debit Dollars if you have put money on your Access (ID) card.

Did You Know?

Block plans are more flexible than traditional meal plans, as meals don't expire at the end of a week or month and are not as rigid about scheduled meals.

Students Speak Out On...
Campus Dining

{

"My brother went to Hopkins, and they have terrible food. So, in light of what other schools have, it's pretty decent here."

Q "The new changes on campus are great. The overall appearance of the dining facilities, specifically the dining hall are wonderful. They bring **a new life to a part of the campus that was in dreadful need of repair**. I think that the changes will attract more and better incoming classes. The students are thrilled about the changes, and the plans for future renovations are exciting."

Q "This is changing, too! Or, so I hope. The food is, in all honesty, okay. The first week you're there, you think, this isn't so bad, and then you stop attempting to be overly cheerful about cafeteria food. You also **learn to avoid the dining hall on weekends**, as it is worse than normal. However, I must include a disclaimer. They're claiming that there's been much improvement to our dining services, so in all possibility, the food's likeability meter could change from okay to pretty good."

Q "I am definitely glad I live off of campus and can cook for myself now. **Pandini's is convenient**, but the D-Hall offers more food. Ben's has better food than the other places, except for Sunday Brunch—nothing beats the brunch."

Q "The D-hall, it's a nice effort but once there are expectations, you must meet them. I think it is actually a step above the food we had, but **the changes are mainly cosmetic**. Jazzman's—love it. I like Pandinis, not my favorite just because I am not a huge pizza fan, but their salads are good. I also love Quizno's now that it is open. I do miss CG just because of the options."

Q "There is a lot more variety on campus than there once was. The dining hall serves more options and of better quality, particularly their produce. The **lines are long at lunchtime**, though, at all dining locations, which can be frustrating."

Q "All I can say is that **I definitely liked the food**. Instead of gaining the Freshman 15, I did the Freshman 25. But, now that I'm starting to play sports again, I feel a little better about it all!"

The College Prowler Take On...
Campus Dining

Although most agree that the food is better, with a larger variety and a better presentation, many seem to feel that the trade-offs in terms of space just haven't been worth it. The Common Ground, previously the best place for students to hang out, with its comfy chairs and adequate seating space, has been gutted to make way for Pandini's, a vaguely Italian pizza and pasta lunch stand.

However, the changes at the dining hall are heralded with more optimism. Now there is make-your-own stir-frys and waffles, omelettes with a staggering array of filling options, and a made-to-order-pasta line. Also added are Sala Rico's and Sky Ranch Grill, with burgers and an American grill menu. The lines aren't any better there at lunch, which is a perennial complaint, and perhaps a testament to the quality of the food. Quizno's now occupies the porch of Marshall-Buchanan hall, which is a student favorite. There is also Jazzman's on the ground floor at the Barnes and Noble bookstore. It is in a prime location for coffee or a muffin before class and is a student hotspot. Again, the lack of space has become a common refrain, with fewer than two dozen seats in the immediate area. Hopefully, as the school gathers feedback on the changes, they will make a corresponding shift in practices.

B

The College Prowler® Grade on

Campus Dining: B

Our grade on Campus Dining addresses the quality of both school-owned dining halls and independent on-campus restaurants as well as the price, availability, and variety of food.

Off-Campus Dining

The Lowdown On...
Off-Campus Dining

Restaurant Prowler:
Popular Places to Eat!

Applebee's

Food: Steak, seafood

2321 Lincoln Highway E.
Lancaster

(717) 290-8330

www.applebees.com

Price: $6–$16 per person

Hours: Sunday–Thursday
11 a.m.–10:30 p.m., Friday–
Saturday 11 a.m.–12:30 a.m.

Blue Pacific Sushi Grill

Food: Japanese

1500 Oregon Pike
Lancaster

(717) 393-9727

www.bluepacificrestaurant.com

Cool Features: Sushi bar,
banquet rooms

Price: $7–$15 (lunch)
$12–$25 (dinner)

Hours: Monday–Thursday
11 a.m.–10 p.m., Friday–
Saturday 11 a.m.–11 p.m.,
Sunday 3:30 p.m.–10 p.m.

Damon's Clubhouse

Food: Steak, seafood, ribs

680 Park City Ctr.
Lancaster

(717) 481-9800

www.damons.com

Cool Features: TVs with sports or an interactive trivia game

Price: $7–$25 per person

Hours: Monday–Thursday 11 a.m.–12 a.m., Friday–Saturday 11 a.m.–1 a.m., Sunday 11 a.m.–10 p.m.

Doc Holliday's

Food: Steak, ribs

931 Harrisburg Pike
Lancaster

(717) 397-3811

www.dhollidays.com

Cool Features: Right across the street from school! Also, the bar is an excellent student hangout for after dinner

Price: $8–$27 per person

Hours: Daily, 11 a.m.–11 p.m. (Bar closes at 1 a.m.)

Eat'n Park

Food: American

1699 Oregon Pike
Lancaster

(717) 390-2212

www.eatnpark.com

Cool Features: Open for all of your late-night coffee and pie needs

Price: $5–$10 per person

Hours: Daily 24 hours

Friendly's

Food: American

1515 Oregon Pike
Lancaster

(717) 393-3369

www.friendlys.com

Cool Features: Fabulous ice cream and dessert options

Price: $6–12 per person

Hours: Daily, 7 a.m.–11 p.m.

Gibraltar

Food: Seafood, fine dining

931 Harrisburg Pike, Lancaster

(717) 397-2790

www.gibraltargrille.com

Cool Features: Right across from the school, Gibraltar's is the perfect place to take your parents when you want a really posh experience without any driving

Price: $18–$32 per person

Hours: Monday–Friday Lunch 11:30 a.m.–2:30 p.m., Monday–Saturday Dinner 5 p.m.–10 p.m. (or 11 p.m.), Sunday 4:30 p.m.–9:30 p.m.

Isaac's Restaurant & Deli

Food: Sandwiches, salads

1559 Manheim Pike
Lancaster

(717) 560-7774

www.isaacsdeli.com

Cool Features: Menu items are named after birds, and a pink flamingo is their trademark symbol

Price: $6–$8 per person

(Isaac's Restaurant & Deli, continued)

Hours: Monday–Saturday
10 a.m.-10 p.m.,
Sunday 11 a.m.–9 p.m.

Lancaster Dispensing Co.

Food: Steak, sandwiches
33 N. Market St.
Lancaster
(717) 299-4602
www.dispensingco.com
Cool Features: Overstuffed
and open-faced sandwiches,
live local music
Price: $5–$15 per person
Hours: Monday–Saturday
11 a.m.–12 p.m., Sunday
12 p.m.–9 p.m.

Lancaster Malt Brewing Co.

Food: American
312 N. Plum St., Lancaster
(717) 391-6258
www.lancasterbrewing.com
Cool Features: Locally
brewed beer, the best
Chicago-style pizza around
Price: $10–$20 per person
Hours: Sunday–Thursday
11:30 a.m.–12 a.m.,Friday–
Saturday 11:30 a.m.–2 a.m.

Lemon Grass Thai Restaurant

Food: Thai
2481 Lincoln Highway E.
Lancaster
(717) 295-1621
www.thailemongrass.com

(Lemon Grass Thai Restaurant, continued)

Cool Features: Fabulous food,
heavenly mango juice, across
the street from Rockvale
Square Outlets, so you can
combine shopping and lunch
Price: $8–$20 per person
Hours: Sunday–Thursday
11:30 a.m.–9 p.m., Friday–
Saturday 11:30 a.m.–10 p.m.

Lily's On Main

Food: American
124 E. Main St.
Ephrata
(717) 738-2711
*www.dhollidays.com/
lilysonmain*
Cool Features: Lite fare is
available, as well as several
lovely salads for the carb-wary
Price: $16–$30 per person
Hours: Monday–Saturday
Lunch 11 a.m.–3 p.m.,
Dinner 5 a.m.–10 p.m.
Sunday Brunch 11 a.m.–3 p.m.,
Dinner 4 p.m.–9 p.m.

Log Cabin Restaurant

Food: American, fine dining
11 Lehoy Forest Dr.
Leola
(717) 626-1181
www.logcabinrestaurant.com
Cool Features: Banquet rooms
available, school events
sometimes held here
Price: $20–$50 per person

(Log Cabin Restaurant, continued)

Hours: Monday–Saturday
5 p.m.–10 p.m.,
Sunday 4 p.m.–9 p.m.

Lyndon City Line Diner

Food: American

1360 Manheim Pike
Lancaster

(717) 393-4878

Cool Features: Classic
diner with better-than-
average coffee

Price: $3–$11 per person

Hours: Always open, except
closed Monday nights from
11 p.m.–5 a.m.

Ming Court Buffet

Food: Chinese

1858 Fruitville Pike
Lancaster

(717) 560-0998

Cool Features: Hundred-item
seafood buffet

Price: $6–$15 per person

Hours: Sunday–Thursday
11 a.m.–9:30 p.m., Friday–
Saturday 11 a.m.–10:30 p.m.

Olive Garden

Food: Italian

910 Plaza Blvd.
Lancaster

(717) 299-2202

www.olivegarden.com

(Olive Garden, continued)

Cool Features: Right next to
Borders for convenient time-
killing during the inevitable
wait for a table

Price: $8–$17 per person

Hours: Sunday–Thursday
11 a.m.–10 p.m., Friday–
Saturday 11 a.m.–11 p.m.

Panera Bread

Food: Sandwiches, salad, soup

2072 Fruitville Pike
Lancaster

(717) 569-5990

www.panerabread.com

Cool Features: Wireless
Internet inside

Price: $6–$9 per person

Hours: Monday–Saturday
6:30 a.m.–9 p.m.,
Sunday 7:30 a.m.–8 p.m.

Papa John's Pizza

1314 Lititz Pike.
Lancaster

(717) 397-7200

Cool Features: Delivery

Price: $7–$17 per person

Hours: Sunday–Thursday
11 a.m.–11 p.m., Friday–
Saturday 11 a.m.–12 a.m.

The Pressroom Restaurant

Food: American

26-28 W. King St.
Lancaster

(717) 399-5400

www.pressroomrestaurant.com

(The Pressroom Restaurant, continued)

Cool Features: Decorated in historical press clippings, dating from the mid-1700s

Price: $7–$13 (lunch) $20–$30 (dinner)

Hours: Monday–Saturday Lunch 11:30 a.m.–3 p.m., Tuesday–Thursday and Sunday Dinner 5 p.m.–9 p.m., Friday–Saturday 5 p.m.–10:30 p.m.

Stockyard Inn Restaurant

Food: Upscale American

1147 Lititz Pike, Lancaster

(717) 394-7975

www.stockyardinn.com

Cool Features: Vegetarian and kids menus available, used to be owned by James Buchanan

Price: $18–$25 per person

Hours: Lunch Tuesday–Friday 11:30 a.m.–2 p.m.; dinner Monday–Thursday 4 p.m.– 9 p.m., Friday–Saturday 4 p.m.–9:30 p.m.

Strawberry Hill

Food: American, fine dining

128 W. Strawberry St. Lancaster

(717) 299-9910

www.strawberryhill restaurant.com

Cool Features: Wine list includes over 1,400 selections

Price: $14–$34 per person

Hours: Daily 5 p.m.–10 p.m.

Taj Mahal Indian Restaurant

Food: Indian

2080 Bennett Ave. Lancaster

(717) 295-1434

www.tajlancaster.com

Cool Features: Live Indian music on weekends

Price: $9–$20 per person

Hours: Daily 5 p.m.–9 p.m.

Thomas Campus Deli

40 Harrisburg Park Lancaster

(717) 509-7700

Cool Features: Eat in, take-out

Price: $5–$8 per person

Hours: Daily 11 a.m.–11 p.m.

Tobias S. Frogg

Food: Sandwiches, salads

1766 Columbia Ave. Lancaster

(717) 394-8366

www.tobiasfrogg.com

Cool Features: Unique specialty drinks, live acoustic music on weekends

Price: $7–$30

Hours: Monday–Tuesday 11 a.m.–12 a.m., Wednesday– Saturday 11 a.m.–2 a.m., Sunday 4 p.m.–11 p.m.

Tokyo Diner
Food: Japanese
1625 Manheim Pike
Lancaster
(717) 569-4305
Cool Features: Sushi bar,
Hibachi grill
Price: $7–$35 per person
Hours: Daily 11 a.m.–10 p.m.

Waffle House
Food: Breakfast
1021 Dillerville Rd
Lancaster
(717) 293-9036
Cool Features: Close
to campus, open for
late-night snacks
Price: $4–$10 per person
Hours: Daily 24 hours

Wish You Were Here
Food: Sandwiches, salads
108 W. Orange St.
Lancaster
(717) 299-5157
www.wishyouwereherepa.com
Price: $3–$6 per person
Hours: Wednesday–Sunday
8 a.m.–1:30 p.m.

Other Places to Check Out:
Brothers & Sisters Cafe
Carlos & Charlie's
Bar & Restaurant
Carribean Breeze Restaurant
My Place Pizzeria
Senorita Burrita
Taco Bell
TGI Friday's

Did You Know?

During First-Year Orientation, **F&M invites local restaurants to set up stands on the Green** so new Fummers can experience the range of what Lancaster has to offer.

Downtown's Central Market, which has its hottest hours on Tuesday and Saturday mornings, offers an assortment of local delicacies, from meats and cheeses to shoo-fly pie and fresh-from-the-cow milk. A must-visit! **It's at the corner of King and Queen Streets**, within walking distance from the college.

Student Favorites:

Isaac's Restaurant & Deli

Tokyo Diner

Wish You Were Here

Closest Grocery Stores:

Huber's West End Market

500 W. Lemon St.

(717) 397-5893

Weis Market

1700 Fruitville Pike

(717) 397-8127

24-Hour Eating:

Eat'n Park

Lyndon City Line Diner

Waffle House

Best Pizza:

Papa John's Pizza

Best Chinese:

Ming Court Buffet

Best Breakfast:

Lyndon City Line Diner

Best Wings:

Lancaster Dispensing Co.

Best Place to Take Your Parents:

Gibraltar

Students Speak Out On...
Off-Campus Dining

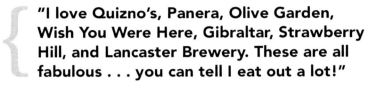

"I love Quizno's, Panera, Olive Garden, Wish You Were Here, Gibraltar, Strawberry Hill, and Lancaster Brewery. These are all fabulous . . . you can tell I eat out a lot!"

Q "Lancaster has some amazing restaurants. It's definitely one of the best parts about the city. I love this restaurant called Tobias Frogg. They have this amazing froggy drink with dry ice that actually bubbles like it's in a bog! The atmosphere is also really nice, and **it's big—a great place for groups**. If you want to go somewhere snazzy with your parents, I'd suggest the Pressroom. I love the fact that they have all these old issues of the *Lancaster Intelligencer* framed on the walls. It's pricey, though, so don't go on your own. For lunch, I like heading down to Central Market. There are all sorts of different types of food (sandwiches, Mexican, baked goods, cheese), and it's all high quality and fresh."

Q "There are **some good places around town**: Wish You Were Here, Brothers & Sisters, Caribbean Breeze."

Q "There are **some pretty great restaurants off campus**. There is Taco Bell, Papa John's, and Chuck E. Cheese."

Q "They're pretty average; **most are the same you'd have anywhere else**. Thomas Campus Deli is close and good; plus there are some really cool places in town like Wish You Were Here."

Q "Local restaurants: Campus Deli (close by, good food, a lot of it), Isaac's (quirky and fun, yummy pretzel bread), My Place (pretty good pizza and big TVs), and there's also a barbeque place nearby that looks fantastic. I've been meaning to try it out. There are lots of places I haven't been—**go exploring**!"

Q "There are a lot of good, off-campus restaurants; in the city, there is Strawberry Hill. Also, students go to **My Place Pizzeria for spaghetti pizza**, which is a Fummer must-eat."

Q "**Off-campus dining is good**. Thomas Campus Deli is open late, and Isaac's is good, too."

Q "Restaurants off campus are great. I generally eat off campus three to four times a week. Some good spots would be Tokyo Diner, Panera, Isaac's, Carlos & Charlie's, My Place, and also the typical chains, Friday's, Olive Garden, Damon's. There are **great places to eat, and they all range in costs**. I would have to say my favorite place to eat is Tokyo Diner—the sushi is fantastic!"

Q "My friends and I are big on desserting since it can get expensive to eat in off-campus restaurants, but we still want to get out and enjoy the town and the different atmospheres. We'll go out just for dessert so our cost is a little more reasonable. **There are so many interesting places to go downtown**. Literally, the best thing to do is just wander until you find an atmosphere that suits you."

Q "**Tokyo Diner for sushi lovers like me**! I also like Isaac's, Panera, Doc's, Papa John's, My Place, and of course, Waffle House if you're just coming from the frats!"

The College Prowler Take On...
Off-Campus Dining

Students relish exploring the off-campus dining opportunities. Whether or not they have a car, students seem to find new gems and old favorites with ease. Food in Lancaster is a serious business for Franklin & Marshall students!

Lancaster seems to have a limitless supply of small, charming restaurants, as well as a fully-stocked range of major restaurant chains. Pizza, Chinese, and sushi restaurants have free delivery to campus and the surrounding area. The local diners, such as the Lyndon Diner, Waffle House, and Eat'n Park, become student favorites during Reading Days for the bottomless coffee cups and all-night hours.

The College Prowler® Grade on
Off-Campus
Dining: B

A high Off-Campus Dining grade implies that off-campus restaurants are affordable, accessible, and worth visiting. Other factors include the variety of cuisine and the availability of alternative options (vegetarian, vegan, Kosher, etc.).

Campus Housing

The Lowdown On...
Campus Housing

Undergrads Living on Campus:
66%

Best Dorm:
Weis Hall

Worst Dorms:
North and South Ben Franklin
Thomas Hall

Number of Dormitories:
9 Dorms
4 Special Interest Houses

Number of University-Owned Apartments:
1

➜

Dormitories:

Ben Franklin Hall North (Mull, Muhlenberg, Rauch, Schaeffer)

Floors: 3 + basement

Total Occupancy: 250

Bathrooms: 1 per hall

Coed: Yes, but single-sex living is available

Residents: Freshmen (Schaeffer and Rauch) and upperclassmen

Room Types: Doubles, singles, one 5-person suite

Special Features: Laundry, large meeting room, kitchenette with sink and microwave in every hall, study rooms, individual rooms are larger than most dorms

Ben Franklin Hall South (Atlee, Dubbs, Klein, Kunkel)

Floors: 3 + basement

Total Occupancy: 202

Bathrooms: 1 per hall (3-4 per floor)

Coed: Yes; but single-sex living is available

Residents: Freshmen (Atlee and Dubbs) and upperclassmen

Room Types: Doubles, singles, one 5-person suite

Special Features: Laundry, kitchenette with sink and microwave in every hall, study rooms, individual rooms are larger than most dorms

Buchanan Halls

Floors: 3 + basement

Total Occupancy: 90

Bathrooms: 1 per floor

Coed: Yes, but basement is single-sex male upperclassmen only

Residents: Mostly freshmen

Room Types: Doubles, basement singles

Special Features: Basement quiet living, laundry, large meeting room, kitchenette with sink and microwave in every hall, connected to Marshall

Community Outreach House

Floors: 3

Total Occupancy: 22

Bathrooms: 1 per floor

Coed: Yes

Residents: Upperclassmen

Room Types: Doubles, singles

Special Features: Community living for students devoted to service, substance-free living, laundry, kitchen with a stove, oven, and refrigerator, recreation/meeting room with study carrels and Ping-Pong

Dietz Hall

Floors: 3

Total Occupancy: 60

Bathrooms: 1 per floor

Coed: Yes

Residents: Upperclassmen

Room Types: Doubles, singles

(Dietz Hall, continued)

Special Features: Laundry, Substance-free living, kitchenettes with a sink, stove, oven, and refrigerator on each floor

French House

Floors: 3

Total Occupancy: 6

Bathrooms: 1 per floor

Coed: Yes

Residents: Upperclassmen

Room Types: doubles, singles

Special Features: Community living for students interested in the French language/culture; laundry, kitchen with a stove, oven, refrigerator; living room

International House

Floors: 2

Total Occupancy: 14

Bathrooms: 1 per floor

Coed: Yes

Residents: Upperclassmen

Room Types: Doubles, singles

Special Features: Community living for international students or students interested in global life; laundry; kitchen with stove, oven, refrigerator, living room, dining/study room, recreation room, basement lounge

Marshall Hall

Floors: 3

Total Occupancy: 90

Bathrooms: 1 per floor

Coed: Yes

Residents: Freshmen

Room Types: Doubles

Special Features: Laundry, large meeting room, kitchenette with sink and microwave in every hall, connected to Buchanan

Murray Arts House

Floors: 3

Total Occupancy: 24

Bathrooms: 1 per floor

Coed: Yes

Residents: Upperclassmen

Room Types: Doubles, singles

Special Features: Community living for students interested in the arts, laundry, kitchen with a stove, oven, refrigerator, recreation room, living room/art studio

Schnader Hall North

Floors: 3 + basement

Total Occupancy: 100

Bathrooms: 1 per floor

Coed: Yes

Residents: Mostly freshmen

Room Types: Doubles

Special Features: Laundry, large meeting room, kitchenette with sink and microwave in every hall, study rooms

Schnader Hall South

Floors: 3 + basement

Total Occupancy: 100

Bathrooms: 1 per floor

Coed: Yes, by floors

Residents: Freshmen

Room Types: Doubles

Special Features: Laundry, large meeting room, kitchenette with sink and microwave in every hall, study rooms

Thomas Hall

Floors: 4

Total Occupancy: 171

Bathrooms: Two per floor

Coed: Yes, by suite

Residents: Upperclassmen

Room Types: 4- and 5-person suites with lounges

Special Features: Laundry, kitchenettes with sinks on each floor, main lounge on the first floor, group study/meeting rooms on each floor

Weis Hall

Floors: 3

Total Occupancy: 150

Bathrooms: 4 per floor

Coed: Yes

Residents: Upperclassmen

Room Types: Doubles, singles, 4-person suites

Special Features: Quiet living on west side, laundry, music practice rooms, floor lounges with TVs, conference room and formal living room (the Fishbowl), kitchenettes with sinks and microwaves, private study cubicles

West James Street Apartments

Floors: 1 floor, 12 apartments

Total Occupancy: 20

Bathrooms: One per apartment

Coed: Yes

Residents: Upperclassmen

Room Types: Doubles, singles, 3-person suites

Special Features: Utilities (except trash pickup) not included, open during holiday breaks, has bathroom, kitchen, common room

Room Types

Doubles; singles; and 3-, 4-, and 5-person suites (composed of a combination of double and single rooms joined by a common area). First-year students are always put into double rooms with a roommate. All of the buildings and most of the halls are coed, and residents are free to make their bathrooms single-sex or coed as they desire, according to their own, student-administered hall standards.

Cleaning Service?

None

What You Get

Each apartment comes with kitchen with oven, stove, and refrigerator; basic living room and bedroom furniture; and a campus computer and telephone connection. You pay for your own power and gas. Laundry services are not available.

Also Available

College Hill and the Lofts aren't college affiliated, so they won't do for your first and second years, but they are nice for your junior or senior year.

Did You Know?

Weis is **the newest dorm**, built in 1989.

Dietz Hall has **full kitchens** on every floor, with a fridge, stove, and microwave.

Every room on campus includes a **free Ethernet connection**.

All dormitories and campus buildings are **smoke-free**.

Students Speak Out On...
Campus Housing

"Dorm life needs to be improved—avoid Ben Franklin. Hopefully, the upcoming house system will improve dorm life."

"Some dorms are pretty nice; I lived in Weis this year (upperclassman housing), which my friends and I referred to as the high-rent district, in comparison to the tenement housing of South Ben. **It's pretty gross in the Ben Franklin housing**. I'm glad I've never lived there."

"Avoid all the dorms—**they are all awful. Weis is probably the nicest of them all**. The Bens are the worst, but they all are bad. They are small, ugly, and have bathrooms that are far away and halls that are too big. But it's just a place to crash; it's not that important. The rest of campus is beautiful, so even when you're putting in your mandatory time in Schnader, it doesn't phase you."

"Dorm life is kind of cool living with so many people your age, but there is almost no privacy. **Marshall-Buch is pretty nice and clean**, and so is Weis. Schnader and the Bens are pretty disgusting, and Thomas is just really loud."

"For freshman dorms, Schnader, Marshall, and Buchanan are good, and for upperclassmen: Thomas or Weis. Avoid the Ben, **they're old and need to be renovated**, and avoid Dietz."

"The dorms are like the food—not bad. But I feel that **it really depends on your hall** to make or break the dorm experience for you."

Q "I have a fond place in my heart for Schnader. The rooms/furniture are pretty nice, depending on what you do to them. **It can feel a bit cramped**, but other than that, I enjoyed living there, for the most part. The absolute worse thing about Schnader is that there are only five or six washing machines for the largest concentrated freshman population."

Q "The dorms are dorms. They aren't worth the money that we pay for them, but I guess it could be worse. There are a few good buildings to be in, mainly the new ones or the newly renovated ones. The rooms are generally on the smaller side, and the furniture isn't so great, but it's not uncomfortable or poor. The kitchens suck in the sense that **they only have a microwave and you can't actually cook in them**. The bathrooms are all communal, which can be good or bad depending on whether it's coed or single gender. Single gender bathrooms tend to be cleaner [Writer's note: Spoken by a woman]."

Q "**Dorms to avoid would most definitely be both North and South Ben, and also Thomas**. The Bens are the oldest dorms, and you can tell that by the conditions of the rooms. It's just sort of gross. Thomas is the party dorm, and while the rooms are dirty and small, there is almost always constant noise, too. Weis is the best dorm to be in. It's quiet and also the cleanest since it's the newest. Schnader isn't a bad dorm; it's pretty clean, but the building is also filled with freshmen, so that makes living a bit loud. The same goes for Marshall-Buchanan. That's an all-freshman dorm, but as a freshman I would suggest those two over the freshman halls in North and South Ben—at least the buildings are clean."

Q "I lived in the old dorms last year and loved them. I think that **it's really hard to find a bad dorm** on this campus."

Q "Dietz is convenient because it's **right in the middle of campus** and provides a kitchen to its residents."

The College Prowler Take On...
Campus Housing

First-year students are given a roommate based on a compatibility questionnaire and are housed in Marshall, Buchanan, Schnader, or one of the Bens. All but the Bens have movable and loftable furniture and are the largest rooms on campus. The faults of the dorms are more evident at the end of the year, when irresponsible, drunken students have had a chance to wreck them.

Many students stay on campus happily all four years at F&M. Weis and Thomas are particularly popular because the suites they offer allow friends to stay together in close proximity. The two couldn't be more different, however. Weis is extremely quiet, and Thomas is extremely loud. Every hall also has a Resident Assistant, who is paid for their services as counselor/supervisor. Competition for these positions is usually high, as they live in a double room by themself. Many who choose to leave the dorms do so for special-interest houses or the West James Apartments. The special interest houses are a wonderful option for community living. Applications are competitive, but not impossible for the right candidates. The apartments are close to campus and are roughly equivalent to non-campus apartments of the same price.

The College Prowler® Grade on

Campus Housing: C+

A high Campus Housing grade indicates that dorms are clean, well-maintained, and spacious. Other determining factors include variety of dorms, proximity to classes, and social atmosphere.

Off-Campus Housing

The Lowdown On...
Off-Campus Housing

Undergrads in Off-Campus Housing:

34%

For Assistance Contact:

Beyond College Avenue

http://server1.fandm.edu/ campusLife/BCA

Best Time to Look for a Place:

Mid-October for a lease that begins the following June 1

Average Rent For:

Studio Apt.: $400/month

1BR Apt.: $450/month

2BR Apt.: $800/month

Popular Areas:

College Hill Apartments

Lemon Street

Pine Street

Walnut Street

West James Street

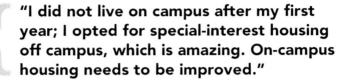

Students Speak Out On...
Off-Campus Housing

> **"I did not live on campus after my first year; I opted for special-interest housing off campus, which is amazing. On-campus housing needs to be improved."**

Q "I don't think sophomores can live off campus, but if you're off campus, it's not too far away because there isn't a lot to do anyway. **It depends on what you want, need, or can afford**."

Q "It's cheaper and nicer than any of the dorms, but beware of the slumlord. I've known students without heat or hot water for the entirety of the winter months. If you get a bad landlord, you need to complain, in writing, and keep a lot of records. Then, you can call the housing inspector if it still isn't fixed. When I moved into my apartment, the fridge wasn't functioning, and **the kitchen ceiling was literally falling down**. But once we got all that fixed, I have had a wonderful off-campus living experience. Our apartment is a lot bigger than any of the dorms, and it has a nice homey feel. We are also responsible for ourselves, which is nice. It's also great to have a place to stay in Lancaster year-round, because you often want to return to campus during breaks to take care of something for a club, or attend a party."

Q "Things to look out for when renting are off-street parking (if you don't have this, street cleaning will ticket you every time); appliances (you don't want to have to bring your own); and a local landlord who is responsive to your concerns. **You also want to pick good roommates who will hang out with you a lot**, otherwise you might feel isolated."

Q "It is so worth it to have your own place and **make your own rules and your own food.** Plus, it works out to be cheaper if you get a reasonably priced place."

Q "I recommend juniors and seniors live off campus. I stayed on campus my junior year, and most of my friends moved off campus that year, so it was harder to visit them. Then, you see your friends with apartments and homes and you're like, 'Wow, **it's a drag to live on campus.**'"

Q "Most of the apartment housing around the campus is mainly occupied by students. Because we're right downtown, **it's fairly easy to get an apartment.** One of the best ways to find a place is to get it after your upperclassmen friend moves out. With a few roommates, I think it's reasonably affordable."

Q "What I've found is some groups (sports teams, frats, clubs) pass their apartments down to lower classmen. This is how I got my current apartment. It works because the older students who have lived off campus before are often living with people living in an apartment for the first time in their lives. It just **helps the new people get acquainted.**"

Q "I'm not a huge fan of communal living, so I'd much rather live in an apartment off-campus with a roommate. It's actually cheaper than on-campus housing sometimes, and it's just nicer. You are able to decorate how you want and clean things so they are actually clean. There are **a bunch of places to rent from** that are right near campus (either across the street or just a few blocks away), and all the landlords are pretty nice. They deal with college students all the time. I've never heard anyone complain about living off campus, whereas people always complain about living on it. Also, I feel like a good percentage of people move off campus after their sophomore year just because of the conditions of the dorms."

The College Prowler Take On...
Off-Campus Housing

Students look forward to their move off campus. The only complaints tend to be about isolation from the campus community. But, if the off-campus resident is careful to read his or her e-mail and stays on campus during the day, he or she can stay in the loop. Rents are reasonable and housing is adequate. The cost of living off campus tends to be slightly lower than living on, but only if the new apartment owner is frugal. Furniture, household costs, and bills can overwhelm you!

Begin your search early, particularly for reliable and tidy roommates. It's best to ask your older friends about their landlords or apartments. Seniors are often happy to know who is inheriting their place. Remember, only juniors and seniors have the option of true off-campus living, although many juniors prefer to live in suites on campus. However, if you're itching for a stove and fridge of your own, moving off campus is a viable option.

The College Prowler® Grade on Off-Campus Housing: A-

A high grade in Off-Campus Housing indicates that apartments are of high quality, close to campus, affordable, and easy to secure.

Diversity

The Lowdown On...
Diversity

Native American:
Less than 1%

White:
82%

Asian American:
4%

International:
8%

African American:
2%

Out-of-State:
65%

Hispanic:
3%

Political Activity

Although the College Republicans have a strong showing on this campus, most of the political activity has been quite liberal. The College Democrats, Students Committed to Social Change, and Environmental Action Alliance have really coalesced and organized a number of complementary events such as getting Fairly Traded coffees on campus, getting F&M to join an anti-sweatshop group, getting students registered to vote, and so forth.

Gay Pride

The gay scene on campus is decent for a fairly conservative campus. The girls interact with Millersville University, a larger school nearby, more so than most other students, but that results in a large dating pool. The boys tend to gravitate to townies at the three local gay or gay-friendly clubs, but dating on campus isn't unheard of. The LGBTA (Lesbian, Gay, Bisexual, Transgender and their Allies) is active.

The LGBTA sponsors weekly discussion groups on a variety of topics, several movie nights per semester in the Allies Resource Center, and their lovely new TV/VCR/DVD player given by GALA, the Gay and Lesbian Alumni Association. Their major events are the National Coming Out Day in October and the National Day of Silence in April, one a day of celebration and the other is a day of protest. They garner several hundred signatures of support from the campus community at each event. During the Day of Silence, over a hundred students, faculty, staff, and administration participate or publicly demonstrate their support.

Most Popular Religions

Judaism, Catholicism, Protestantism, Islam, Unitarian Universalist, Orthodox Christian, and Buddhist: we've got it all! Hillel House and a few campus Christian groups are the most active, although the Freethinkers, an agnostic/atheistic group, have a strong following, as well.

Economic Status

Working-class students keep their heads down here at F&M, as the parking lot full of Beamers and Volvos will attest. Trust-fund Trixies and Trevors will find themselves right at home, however. The students at F&M tend to be sheltered, suburban, and well-to-do, although there are a number of students with broader experiences or less cash. But those latter keep a much lower profile. Public high school experiences are more common than private, however, and the upper-middles should be comfortable here, as well.

Minority Clubs

Minority clubs make a respectable showing here at F&M, collaborating extensively for major events, as well as their own, more personal weeks and months. Latino Heritage Month kicks things off in October, with daily events and speakers, closing with a heck off a party in the International House from Mi Gente Latina. The BSU hosts a Step Show every February, as part of Black History Month events. Sangam and the Asian Cultural Society host Diwali and Mabuhay, respectively—the most well-attended events on campus. Indian dancing and food attract what feels like the entire campus, and the International Club (I-Club) parties pull almost as heavy a crowd.

Students Speak Out On...
Diversity

> **"I feel that our campus is diverse in international students and not as diverse with U.S. minority students. There are tons of students from Turkey, Bulgaria, and more."**

Q "Is F&M diverse? Not particularly. Being one of the 50 or so black people on campus was a definite adjustment. The numbers are not the really hard part; **it's the attitudes of the majority, which are stifling**. F&M is not a place where I have felt supported or flourish like I might have at a more diverse, liberal school. I have survived it, and in the process learned some really important things about myself and others. College is all about self growth, and F&M has certainly made me a stronger person."

Q "F&M has been dubbed **the place diversity comes to die** for a reason."

Q "You need to look for diversity. The campus really isn't, though **it makes great efforts to be diverse**."

Q "Well, **the administration gets its boxers in a bunch over this one quite often**. Yes, the campus is predominately white. We have a significant Hispanic/Latino population, as well as an African American one. There are quite a few international students, mostly from Eastern countries (Pakistan, India) and Eastern Europe (Bulgaria). We also have a strong Jewish population. We also have an active gay/lesbian/bisexual/ally community."

Q "I hate these kind of breakdowns of the student population. Personally, everyone should stop worrying about color/race/religion/sexuality and start caring about the people. I understand that people identify with those who are most like them; however, this conscious/subconscious grouping of the student population can also be harmful in that no one really does diversify. To me, diversity is not merely the presence of different cultural/lifestyle (shudder) groups, but the integration of those groups with each other and with the entire campus population. I would love to see a community where differences are both respected and accepted, not where they can be barriers. **Everyone is part of a community here**."

Q "I think to truly succeed in building a 'diverse' campus, and not just a diverse campus but a close-knit one, **we should focus on stressing everyone's common identity**. They are part of the F&M community, which is a common identity shared not only with students, but with administrators, professors, and staff."

Q "Campus is diverse, but **most of the minorities seem to choose to hang out with people of their own race**. I don't think anyone is to blame. That's just what they choose to do."

Q "It's really not that diverse, even though we have clubs that represent all the different ethnicities and races that are on campus, so **I guess we are sort of diverse**."

Q "The school is not diverse as much as it could be, but **diversity is really what you make of it**. The more you make friends with people from different areas and nationalities, the more diverse your experience will be here."

The College Prowler Take On...
Diversity

Every other week, a forum called Race Matters is hosted by a sociology professor and a history professor, and pulls interested members of the campus community (of all races and ethnicities) to discuss current events as it relates to race. These discussions happen more frequently as the F&M community faces the racial tensions that face all Americans who want to live in a richer, more diverse community. Franklin & Marshall is facing its problems straight on, but facing them and healing them are two separate things entirely.

Thankfully, there have been few major racial incidents of late, but those slurs that occur are always greeted with howls of dismay from all members of the campus community and official, rapid opprobrium from the Powers That Be. We can only hope that F&M's efforts to widen horizons and open doors are paying off for its students.

The College Prowler® Grade on
Diversity: D-

A high grade in Diversity indicates that ethnic minorities and international students have a notable presence on campus and that students of different economic backgrounds, religious beliefs, and sexual preferences are well-represented.

Guys & Girls

The Lowdown On...
Guys & Girls

Men Undergrads:
53%

Women Undergrads:
47%

Most Prevalent STDs on Campus

Chlamydia, herpes

Birth Control Available?

Condoms are free at Appel Infirmary and the Women's Center, and prescriptions for birth-control pills and the morning-after pill are available.

Social Scene

While a number of students meet their Mr. or Ms. Right Now at a party, many Fummers do find a soul mate on campus. Traditional dates are less common than group dates or simply "hanging out."

Hookups or Relationships?

Both happen, though you're much more likely to find a hookup at a frat party than you are a significant other. Surprisingly enough, drunken debauchery doesn't lend itself to serious commitment. What are the odds?

Best Way to Meet Guys/Girls

In class, at club meetings, or through friends—the same way you'd meet any new friend.

Dress Code

Franklin and Marshall is a fairly preppy school, so Polo shirts and khakis for both sexes when they're dressing up for work. But when it's an 8 a.m. class, expect only pajama pants and F&M sweatshirts.

Did You Know?

Top Places to Find Hotties:

1. Steinman College Center
2. Ben's Underground
3. On the Green or Quad on sunny days

Top Places to Hook Up:

1. Basement of Shadek-Fackenthal Library
2. Greenhouse on the roof of Fackenthal Laboratories
3. Frat party
4. Weis Fishbowl
5. Your room, but sexile your roommate first!

Students Speak Out On...
Guys & Girls

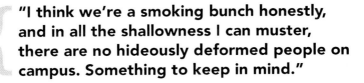

"I think we're a smoking bunch honestly, and in all the shallowness I can muster, there are no hideously deformed people on campus. Something to keep in mind."

Q "Well, according to my tastes, I can only really comment on the guys. The school tends to be very country clubish, which is most definitely not what I am attracted to. There are good guys around, but you need to look pretty hard for them. **It can be hard to maintain an ordinary relationship** (seeing each other regularly) because there is a lot of work, and I am rather involved on campus. You can definitely make it work, though."

Q "F&M guys are all right. A lot are **kind of sleazy**, but mostly, they are all tolerable. In the looks department, they're all right, but we could use some more hot guys. The girls are all right, but too many of them are too into clothing and looking like money to be easy to handle. But, there are definitely some amazing ones around if you aren't afraid to look."

Q "Most of the guys looked like they came off the Ralph Lauren walkway, but not as hot. **The preppy look is in here**, just flip through the pages of J.Crew and Gap and you'll see F&M students in it. The same goes for the girls, me being one of them."

Q "**Dating on campus is very conservative**. It seems like all the guys are looking for someone to marry, which can be a lot of pressure on an independent, college-aged woman. There is a good deal of random hooking up, but any dating relationship seems to get very serious, very fast, and is generally overly traditional."

Q "For the most part, **guys and girls are preppy and financially stable**, although there is also a liberal undertow on campus that enriches the student body. I think guys at F&M are hot; well, hotter than the girls at F&M."

Q "The girls aren't as bad as everyone says they are. Just **wish I could find one for me**, though."

Q "The guys are a mix, as are the girls. **You'll find all kinds of different people at F&M** (though very few of different ethnic and racial backgrounds; diversity is not big at this school). There are some great guys and girls at F&M and then again, there aren't; it's hard to say. I love the people I'm friends with and have a great time with them. People are generally really friendly, especially when they've had a bit to drink, so you can almost always find someone to talk to. There are some hot guys, but it's slim pickings. Girls—don't expect to find your soul mate here. As for the girls . . . oh we are so hot!"

Q "F&M's reputation in this area is terribly inaccurate! **We have plenty of hot kids around**. And with four other area colleges to choose from, it's hard to go wrong!"

Q "**The gay girl scene is good here**—everyone is really nice and friendly, and there's a much larger breadth of choice here than you'd expect because of the Girls Only parties every month. Every gay girl in the county comes to one at one time or another, it feels like."

The College Prowler Take On...
Guys & Girls

Franklin & Marshall students tend to lean toward the clean-cut, preppy sort. Few students can complain that there are no hot prospects. The ratio of guys to girls at F&M is about 50/50, so whichever you prefer, your game is plentiful. The girls complain that the guys are self-involved twits, and the guys complain that the girls are self-absorbed airheads, but they continue to go after each other.

It appears to be the case that the guys are dateable if you can put up with video games and backwards baseball caps. The girls are dateable if you can deal with smart girls trying a little too hard to pretend they're not. Hot is relative—we'll never be at UCLA for the sun-bronzed hotties, but we're pretty content with our contents.

The College Prowler® Grade on

Guys: B

A high grade for Guys indicates that the male population on campus is attractive, smart, friendly, and engaging, and that the school has a decent ratio of guys to girls.

The College Prowler® Grade on

Girls: B+

A high grade for Girls not only implies that the women on campus are attractive, smart, friendly, and engaging, but also that there is a fair ratio of girls to guys.

Athletics

The Lowdown On...
Athletics

Athletic Division:
Division III
Division I Wrestling

Conference:
Centennial (CC)
Eastern College Athletic
(ECAC)

School Mascot:
The Diplomat

**Men Playing
Varsity Sports:**
326 (32%)

**Women Playing
Varsity Sports:**
187 (21%)

→

Men's Varsity Teams:

Baseball

Basketball

Cross-Country

Football

Golf

Lacrosse

Soccer

Squash

Swimming & Diving

Tennis

Track & Field
(indoor and outdoor)

Wrestling

Women's Varsity Teams:

Basketball

Cross-Country

Field Hockey

Golf

Lacrosse

Soccer

Softball

Squash

Swimming & Diving

Tennis

Track & Field
(indoor and outdoor)

Volleyball

Club Sports:

Cheerleading

Crew

Cricket

Equestrian

Ice Hockey

Rugby (men, women)

Volleyball (men)

Intramurals:

Basketball (men, women)

Flag Football (men, women)

Soccer

Softball (men, women, coed)

Volleyball (men,
women, coed)

Most Popular Sports

Basketball, rugby, soccer, swimming

Best Place to Take a Walk

Buchanan Park's Rose Garden

Athletic Fields

Sponaugle-Williamson Field

With seating capacity for 4,000 fans, this is the home for Diplomats football and lacrosse programs. Sponaugle-Williamson Field also includes the eight-lane William J. Iannicelli Track. Field events are held in the infield of the track, which includes concrete throwing circles, as well as a javelin approach, high-jump apron, and two-jump runways.

Caplan Field

The fields include dugouts, an outdoor batting tunnel, bullpens, press box, a Nevco scoreboard, and portable grandstand seating. There is a softball field located directly behind it, on Baker Campus, a few blocks off the College's main campus on Harrisburg Pike.

Getting Tickets

Tickets? What tickets? Just show up! F&M fans will gladly make space on the bench for another Diplomat enthusiast.

Overlooked Teams

The football team hasn't had the greatest record in the past, to say the least. Most Dips just wince. But the cheerleading club faithfully cheers them on—when those talented young women aren't out winning contests of their own!

Gyms/Facilities

The Alumni Sports and Fitness Center
The ASFC is a multi-purpose athletic and recreation facility on North Campus (across Harrisburg Pike from the main campus). A 52,000 square-foot field house includes five full-size courts (convertible to basketball, tennis, and volleyball), a six-lane 200-meter track, a fitness center (equipped with strength-training machines and a variety of aerobic equipment), meeting rooms, locker rooms, offices, a catering facility, and a suspended track. The facility also includes an Olympic-size pool with spectator seating and team locker rooms.

Mayser Center
This facility contains the varsity gymnasium, with four traditional-sized and four international squash courts, athletic offices, team locker rooms, a training room, an equipment room and a strength training center, featuring strength training machines and a complete Cybex free-weight system. It holds 3,000 people and has been the site for many conference and NCAA Championship tournament events.

Strength Training Center
The 2,700-square-foot center consists of $100,000 of York Barbell Company's state-of-the-art strength training machines and a complete free weight system.

Students Speak Out On...
Athletics

"IM sports like basketball and softball and club sports like rugby, Frisbee, and crew are very popular. Varsity sports do not get enough attention from students and profs, in my opinion."

Q "Since it's a small school, a lot of people are athletes, so being on a varsity team isn't that big of a deal. **IM sports don't seem particularly active**, but I could be wrong."

Q "I don't pay attention to sports, really. I have nothing to offer here except that **our lacrosse teams are awesome** and the football team isn't."

Q "Varsity sports are kind of in-between. People go to the games, especially basketball, but **life does not revolve around them**. IM sports are also kind of in-between. People play them and people watch them, but they aren't all dominating or anything."

Q "I personally haven't attended varsity sporting events. However, a lot of **students do go to basketball games**. As for IM sports, rugby is very popular, and I, like many students, usually attend these games. Another big IM sport is ultimate Frisbee."

Q **"We have varsity sports**?"

Q "I actually don't know the answer to this since I'm not a sports person. Some people are into sports, and some aren't. **IM sports are decently big on campus**—I always find people participating in them. Also, people always go out to watch the varsity sports games, so I guess that is pretty big, too."

Q "Basketball is big 'cause **they win**."

The College Prowler Take On...
Athletics

Students seem remarkably unaware of the sports scene. And although several teams at F&M have winning seasons, the relatively low profile of varsity sports on campus limits the number of spectators. Teams bend over backwards to boost the number of attendants to their games because students who attend are usually enthusiastic in their support and have fun.

Many F&M students participate in at least one club or intramural sport. However, for those who seek them out, the sports scene thrives. One-third of the guys play a varsity sport, and one-fourth of the women do. The number of intramural players is higher than that. Dips certainly aren't lumps of inactivity, even if they aren't the most spirited fans!

The College Prowler® Grade on

Athletics: C

A high grade in Athletics indicates that students have school spirit, that sports programs are respected, that games are well-attended, and that intramurals are a prominent part of student life.

Nightlife

The Lowdown On...
Nightlife

Club and Bar Prowler: Popular Nightlife Spots!

Chameleon Club

223 N. Water St.

(717) 299-9684

www.chameleonclub.net

Lancaster is kind of hurting for good clubs, so the Chameleon is about as good as it gets. Nightclubbing isn't really F&M students' style for a party. You have to pay a cover and for all your drinks, you have to rub elbows with sketchy

(Chameleon Club, continued)

townies, and you have to walk significantly longer in the dark, not-so-good parts of town than if you were going to the frats or a house party. But, if you're really craving that beat, the Chameleon is where to go. They have a lot of really great live acts like Reel Big Fish, Less than Jake, the Pixies, Modest Mouse, and Weezer have been known to play there, as well as great local bands like School of Athens, the Mint, Ennui, and Lovedrug for no cover.

➔

Alley Kat

30 W. Lemon St.

(717) 509-8686

The Alley Kat is great for a loud bunch who just want watch the Phillies game all night and throw back a few drinks. It's a bit of a walk, but it has a very friendly ambience that rewards the effort.

The Belvedere Inn

402 N. Queen St.

(717) 394-2422

www.belvederepa.com

In search of the perfect apple martini? Look no further. For drinking in style, pick the Belvedere. It's not overloaded with students, but not entirely lacking; the Belvedere is the favorite hangout of the choosier student.

Brendee's Café

449 W. Lemon St.

(717) 397-8646

Brendee's is a student favorite, with darts in the hopping back room and relatively cheap drinks. Brendee's is typically well-lit for a dive of its genre, but that only means that you can see the locals hitting on you all the more clearly. Brendee's is the site of a number of senior class gatherings, as the pitcher specials are a marvel here.

Fulton Bar

637 N. Plum St.

(717) 291-1098

If you're interested in the local Lancaster crowd, the Fulton is the place to be. The fashionable 20-somethings love this downtown bar, although few students venture quite that far from campus. The walk or drive is well-rewarded at this hip hangout.

Quips Pub

457 New Holland Ave.

(717) 397-3903

www.quipspub.com

A British-style pub, Quips has atmosphere hanging off every inch of its wood-panelled walls. A favorite among younger faculty, students frequently find themselves rubbing elbows with their history or philosophy professor.

Tally-Ho Tavern

201 W. Orange St.

(717) 299-0661

A small bar downtown, this is the major local gay hotspot. The close-knit group of mostly men is remarkably friendly, and the 'Ho's karaoke Tuesdays must be heard to be believed.

Student Favorites:

Belvedere Inn

Brendee's Café

Chameleon Club

Bars Close At:

2 a.m.

Local Specialties:

Rolling Rock

Stoudt's

Yuengling

Other Places to Check Out:

Doc's

East of Eden Pub

Encore Lounge

Jukebox Nightclub

Rick's Place

Shamrock Café

Tails Bar & Grill

Favorite Drinking Games:

Beer Laps

Beer Pong

Card Games (A$$hole)

Power Hour

Quarters

Useful Resources for Nightlife

Your best bet is upperclassmen, who are usually more than willing to haul a first-year around to parties, but you could also check out *www.downtownlancaster.com*.

Primary Areas with Nightlife

F&M's east side is the place where anything happens at night, from Harrisburg Pike to Lemon Street and from College Ave. to Charlotte Street.

Cheapest Place to Get a Drink

Frat parties are free, but Brendee's Café offers great pitcher specials.

What to Do if You're Not 21

The Chameleon Club usually admits 18 and over, and the ID checks at frat parties are only for show. You can get in anywhere except the bars. And even then, some places let you in—but I'll let you discover where—it's more fun that way.

Organization Parties

The International Club and Mi Gente Latina throw some of the best parties around (dry only, but you'll have so much fun salsaing, you won't notice). The Blizzard Bash is a fun semi-formal in the winter, and the cultural clubs band together in March or April to throw one hell of a multi-cultural formal at a hotel or art gallery off campus.

Frats

See the Greek section!

Students Speak Out On...
Nightlife

> **"There are not many options for bars and clubs off campus, but you usually run into a lot of fellow Fummers there. Go to Brendee's and Chameleon Club."**

Q "All parties are off campus, as **the club scene off campus is lacking**, and I don't know the bar scene!"

Q "There are **a lot of frat parties**, which I'm not really down for. So, I tend to go to house parties and stuff like that."

Q "The parties on and off campus tend to be pretty good, and almost **all kinds of people can find ones that suit them**."

Q "Most students do not have parties on campus because of housing constraints, so most parties are off campus at personal homes, apartments, or fraternity houses. As for bars, **students of age go to Brendee's**, which is also a fun place for friends to hang out at and have a few drinks after a hard day of classes."

Q "Parties off campus, if you're under 21 and a freshman, are usually frat parties. Pretty much everything you've heard about those are true. Do not fear, non-frat-type partiers! As you make friends, including upperclassmen, you will find **there are more fun parties in apartments**."

Q "Parties are fun; there is generally every type (small, big, loud, quiet, crazy, intellectual). They also happen on the weekends and the weekdays. Really, there is something for everyone, every night of the week. The parties are in the frat houses, dorms (shhh . . . don't tell Public Safety), the special interest houses, and off-campus apartments. The bars are okay. The best part about them is that they are **within walking distance of campus**."

Q "There are parties on campus? Are those allowed—haha. I don't really go to any college-sponsored parties, but the frat parties are great. I know I always have a great time going to those. Also house parties are always fun. **The party life at F&M is great**—it always seems that someone is throwing a party somewhere. As for bars, I don't know about that because I am not 21 yet. And as for clubs, I haven't heard of any good ones, and I don't think that many people go clubbing, or at least many people that I know."

Q "The parties are a lot of fun. This school tends to have **a work hard, play harder mentality**. As for bars, we'll pretend that at 18, I wouldn't know."

Q "**I like going to the frats** more in the fall semester—it's more crowded. I'd rather go to private parties after freshman year, though."

The College Prowler Take On...
Nightlife

Connections are everything when it comes to finding a party. First-years tend to be restricted to fraternity and team parties. But as they find their niche and friends, they grow to be a part of the party community. After their first year, guys must belong to a fraternity or have a friend in one, in order to attend fraternity parties; many choose to do so, as the drinks are free.

There is also a solid core of non-partiers. For while many F&M students work hard and play harder, there are a few that choose to work hard—and then work harder.

The College Prowler® Grade on

Nightlife: C-

A high grade in Nightlife indicates that there are many bars and clubs in the area that are easily accessible and affordable. Other determining factors include the number of options for the under-21 crowd and the prevalence of house parties.

Greek Life

The Lowdown On...
Greek Life

Number of Fraternities:
7

Undergrad Men in Fraternities:
35%

Number of Sororities:
2

Undergrad Women in Sororities:
20%

→

Fraternities on Campus:

Chi Phi

Delta Sigma Phi

Kappa Sigma

Phi Kappa Psi

Phi Kappa Sigma

Phi Kappa Tau

Sigma Pi

Sororities on Campus:

Chi Omega

Kappa Beta Gamma

Other Greek Organizations:

Alumni Greek Council

Greek Council

Interfraternity Council

Panhellenic Council

Did You Know?

Kappa Beta Gamma is a relatively new sorority on campus, which you'll learn, doesn't happen very often.

Students Speak Out On...
Greek Life

"I think for freshmen, frat parties can play a large role, and okay, dominate to a degree. After freshman year, students get more involved with what is going on, on campus and at house parties. With re-recognition, things are changing."

"Unfortunately, yes, **it does dominate life on campus**."

"Greek life? I'm not really a part of it, although some of my friends are and/or desire to be. Quite honestly, I feel as though rush/pledge weeks are significantly more important for males because there is free booze and lots of women. **It's a lot harder for guys to party if they're not a part of a frat**, and that's the type of scene they enjoy being a part of (while still under 21). Sororities are a little bit more low-key, depending on which one you choose to become friends with."

"It's definitely got a strong presence and it is getting stronger. **It does not dominate the social scene**, but it really does aid it."

"Greek life dominates the freshman social scene. There are **free drinks, dancing, and drunken fun** for all to enjoy. But mostly guys decide to pledge, and girls usually do not."

"Greek life **does not dominate my social scene**."

Q "Greek life is fantastic! **I love Greek life**! It makes F&M so much more fun to go to. The relationships that I have with my sisters are just amazing and really are everlasting. As for the social scene, I would definitely say that Greek life dominates it. When people go out to party, 99 percent of the time, they are going to the frat parties. Greeks are just popular and people know them. Also, the fact that we make up about one-third of the student body helps us to keep our social dominance. To be honest though, Greeks tend to be the pretty people— the people who have a lot of money, the people who drink a lot, the people who hook-up a lot, and sometimes, even the people who do drugs a lot. That doesn't mean that all Greeks are that way, but some people certainly fulfill the stereotype. I love Greek life for both its positives and negatives, and I would say that Greek life is even on the rise at F&M. Re-recognition should make things quite interesting."

Q "Greeks may be active on campus (35 percent of men and about 20 percent of women), but **the frat scene is not the be-all-end-all to social life** at F&M. It's hard to explain, and a lot of fun to experience. They aren't your stereotypical frat boys, either!"

Q "I don't think there is any social life for a guy who decides to go non-Greek, unless he's on a team. I think **it's a lot easier on girls who choose to remain GDI**."

The College Prowler Take On...
Greek Life

Fraternities and sororities have been re-recognized by President Fry's administration, following 16 years of official "de-recognition." The greater faculty and administration involvement in Greek life is expected to minimize the risks and pitfalls of the Greek experience, such as hazing, poor grades, and alcohol abuse. They also want to strengthen the bonds between F&M and its Greek students, as well as alumni.

Although not mandatory for a good time, Greek life is predominate at F&M. The heavily publicized frat parties are well-attended, and drunken guys and scantily-clad girls can be seen nearly every night lurking near lettered houses. More than a third of men choose to pledge, and a fourth of women do as well. While they rave about their social experiences, reports of hazing, alcohol abuse, and other dangers of Greek life are as prevalent here as at any Greek Row.

The College Prowler® Grade on

Greek Life: A-

A high grade in Greek Life indicates that sororities and fraternities are not only present, but also active on campus. Other determining factors include the variety of houses available and the respect the Greek community receives from the rest of the campus.

Drug Scene

The Lowdown On...
Drug Scene

Most Prevalent Drugs on Campus:

Aderol, cocaine, marijuana

Liquor-Related Referrals:

123

Liquor-Related Arrests:

2

Drug-Related Referrals:

4

Drug-Related Arrests:

0

Drug Counseling Programs:

Counseling Services
(717) 291-4083

Students Speak Out On...
Drug Scene

"Some people do coke. I have heard of no ecstasy. Some people smoke pot. It doesn't seem to be a pressing problem."

Q "There's **a lot of drinking**, weed (although it seems a lot more visible freshman year), and blow (cocaine)."

Q "I was surprised to see **how big the problem was**."

Q "Yes, **there are drugs here**! As long as a student has a strong fan, he/she can smoke pot undiscovered (sometimes). There are also other drugs like coke and E. But on the whole, most students do not do drugs."

Q "It's present, but it is **mostly pot and alcohol**—what else is new?"

Q "From what I've seen of the drug scene, **I believe it is safe and purely recreational**. This is only my opinion of what I've seen, though."

Q "There is one. I don't really know much more than that. It's not a huge scene, but people do drugs on campus; **it's just a part of life**."

Q "This is a really conservative school, and you can see it by the drugs that the students use. **The drug of choice is definitely pot**. You hardly hear of people doing cocaine or hallucinogens.

Q "It's a little heavier than I expected. Actually, **about 25 percent of fraternity members use cocaine**, but that's 25 percent of 40 percent of the boys on campus. Pot is more common than coke, and Ritalin or Adderall abuse is even more common than pot use (in my experience). But, all-in-all, the drug scene is one that's very avoidable. No one's going to force them down your throat. In fact, you probably won't even see it unless you go looking for it."

The College Prowler Take On...
Drug Scene

F&M runs an intense anti-drug campaign, but statistics on posters don't discourage the truly committed. Marijuana is the most common and easily obtained: simply go upstairs at any frat party and follow your nose. Among the wealthier students, cocaine is an option, but that's rare to find in public. E is something students use during winter vacations to Ibiza or New York City, but not on campus. Prescription drug abuse is rare, but it has been known to happen at times.

By far, the most common drug on campus is GHB: the date-rape drug. Girls—watch your drinks. Don't put them down and expect to drink from them again. If you're careful, you'll be fine. But remember to party in groups, and don't be stupid about taking drinks from people you don't know. The trouble with GBH or "roofies" is that the victim wakes up without knowing what happened the night before. This is a problem at any campus, and there are a couple of fraternity houses at F&M, in particular, to be cautious of. F&M's Red Zone program tries to make first-year women aware of their risk and make sure that they have the resources they need to find help, if necessary.

The College Prowler® Grade on

Drug Scene: B

A high grade in the Drug Scene indicates that drugs are not a noticeable part of campus life; drug use is not visible, and no pressure to use them seems to exist.

Campus Strictness

The Lowdown On...
Campus Strictness

What Are You Most Likely to Get Caught Doing on Campus?
- Being drunk and disorderly
- Downloading copyrighted materials
- Graffit or vandalizing school property
- Illegally parking or recklessly driving

Students Speak Out On...
Campus Strictness

> "Campus police want you to be safe. You can't get away with much, but they are nice people and put safety before busting you."

Q "I don't know of too many people who have **gotten into trouble**."

Q "They are **pretty strict about drugs** but often let drinking slide if you are quiet and not being blatant and harmful to yourself, others, or property."

Q "Campus police are strict on drinking, especially if you're underage. As for drugs, I haven't seen any incidents occur, but **campus police like to 'punish' the underagers for drinking**."

Q "Campus security is honestly here to **keep everyone safe and to keep the peace**."

Q "We have policies about that stuff? **People only get in trouble when they get caught**, and that is when they are being blatant about what they are doing. I would say policies are strict, but most often people never get caught unless they are acting stupid."

Q "As I said, the campus police try hard, but **mostly they don't bust that many people**. Only the dumb ones (belligerently drunk, noisy, barfing people)."

Q "**It's mostly disturbance-driven**. If you are being belligerent and loud, blatantly drunk or high, expect to get caught. But it's really a campus that is more concerned with your safety than what you're doing behind closed doors. The only incident I have had with security was when I was stopped because a female guard was concerned because I was being helped home by two men. In all honesty, it could have been a very bad situation that she was just trying to avert."

Q "It's too strict! I visited some liberal arts schools around our area like Haverford, and their RAs provide residents with alcohol! **Our school demands that the RAs write their residents up**, even if they see them holding an unopened can of beer."

The College Prowler Take On...
Campus Strictness

The Department of Public Safety is disturbance-driven in their stance toward alcohol. They also prefer to run educational programs and self-defense classes to lower the incidences of those disturbances.

Keep your head down and be polite. Then you'll get off with a warning. But don't park in a FSA parking spot, or you'll have your head ripped off and handed to you! We'll have more on this in the next section.

The College Prowler® Grade on

Campus Strictness: B-

A high Campus Strictness grade implies an overall lenient atmosphere; police and RAs are fairly tolerant, and the administration's rules are flexible.

Parking

The Lowdown On...
Parking

Student Parking Lot?
Yes

Freshmen Allowed to Park?
First-year students are no longer permitted to bring cars on campus.

Parking Permit Cost:
Parking permits are free

F&M Parking Services:
Department of Public Safety
(717) 291-3939

Common Parking Tickets:
Not Registered: $10

No Parking or Reserved Zone: $25

Handicapped Zone: $40

Fire Lane: Towing plus $40

Parking Permits

All students are required to register their cars, but it is free. They receive a sticker for the rear windscreen. However, if students do not do this, they will receive a ticket, or could have their car towed.

Did You Know?

Best Places to Find a Parking Spot
ASFC Lot or Secured Lot, both of them at the corner of Harrisburg Pike and Race Avenue

Good Luck Getting a Parking Spot Here!
West Lot, Weis Lot, and Marshall-Buchanan spaces

Students Speak Out On...
Parking

"It is so hard to park! I have my own lot (at the Community Outreach House), otherwise it would be a problem. Freshmen can't bring cars anymore, so that changes things."

Q "**It seems decent enough**. I don't have a car, though."

Q "Just **don't get caught by street cleaning!**"

Q "Parking is **difficult during the week**. If you don't get a good spot during the weekend when people go home, you'll probably end up walking, although not very far."

Q "Trust me, don't bring a car. **You'll walk farther to your space than to the store**."

Q "With first-years **not able to bring their cars**, I can imagine it will be a lot easier to park around campus."

Q "The parking scene sucks on campus. There is a very small parking lot behind North and South Ben and beside Weis. If you're lucky, you can get a spot there. **There is parking along the street behind the dorms**, too. But once again, you have to be lucky to get a spot there."

Q "Parking on the street isn't all that great, though, because you have to remember what day is street- cleaning day so you can move your car and avoid getting a ticket. There is also a parking lot across the street that is gated off. You can generally find spots there and in the back lot at the ASFC. **It's not a problem to park there**, but it sucks when you want to use your car and you have to walk all the way across the street to get it. It's not bad when it's nice out, but in the winter and the rain, it is not so much fun."

The College Prowler Take On...
Parking

Although there are usually sufficient parking spaces for F&M students in the dorms, not all of those spaces are convenient. During special events in the ASFC such as speakers, debates, or Chamber of Commerce dinners, students are required to move their cars, sometimes several blocks away.

Students are only permitted to park on the street in certain places, although it is strongly advised against. Vandalism against F&M students' cars is high. (Where else are you going to get such a nice stereo?) Parking in FSA (Faculty, Staff, and Administration) spots is highly advised against, as Public Safety is not opposed to multiple ticketing during each of their hourly (or more frequent) patrols. It's not unheard of for an illegally parked student to rack up nearly a hundred dollars in fines.

The College Prowler® Grade on

Parking: C

A high grade in this section indicates that parking is both available and affordable, and that parking enforcement isn't overly severe.

Transportation

The Lowdown On...
Transportation

Ways to Get Around Town:

On Campus
F&M's campus is only 170 acres in area—we don't need a campus bus!

Public Transportation
Red Rose Transit Authority (RRTA)
45 Erick Rd.
(717) 397-4246

Taxi Cabs
Friendly Transportation (also Limousine Service)
625 E. Orange St.
(717) 393-6666

Lancaster Yellow Cab & Baggage Inc.
625 E. Orange St.
(717) 397-8100

→

Car Rentals

Alamo
local: (717) 290-1414
national: (800) 327-9633
www.alamo.com

Avis
local: (717) 560-5353
national: (800) 831-2847
www.avis.com

Enterprise
local: (717) 290-1111
national: (800) 736-8222
www.enterprise.com

Hertz
local: (717) 569-2331
national: (800) 654-3131
www.hertz.com

Best Ways to Get Around Town

By foot

Ways to Get Out of Town:

Airports

Lancaster Airport

500 Airport Rd.
Lititz

(717) 569-1221

www.lancasterairport.com

Going east on Harrisburg Pike, turn left onto Queen Street. At the train station (when the road ends), turn left. Bear right, following the signs for Lititz Pike. Airport will be on the right, just out of town.

(Airports, continued)

Harrisburg International Airport (HIA)

208 Airport Dr.
Middletown

(888) 235-9442

www.flyhia.com

Going west on Harrisburg Pike, take Route 30 east to the 283 west exit. Watch for the airport exit after about thirty minutes, before you get into Harrisburg proper.

Airlines Serving Lancaster

US Airways Express
(800) 428-4322
www.usairways.com

Airlines Serving Harrisburg

Air Canada
(888) 247-2262
www.aircanada.ca

American Airlines
(800) 433-7300
www.aa.com

Continental
(800) 523-3273
www.continental.com

Delta
(800) 221-1212
www.delta.com

Northwest
(800) 225-2525
www.nwa.com

TWA
(800) 221-2000
www.twa.com

→

(Airlines Serving Harrisburg, continued)

United
(800) 241-6522
www.united.com

US Airway
 (800) 428-4322
www.usairways.com

How to Get to the Airport

A cab ride to Lancaster Airport costs no more than $10, but to Harrisburg usually costs about $50. The train is less than $15.

Capital Trailways
53 McGovern Ave.
(717) 397-4861

Amtrak
53 McGovern Ave.
(800) USA-RAIL

Greyhound
53 E. Mcgovern Ave.
(717) 397-4861

Travel Agents
AAA Travel Agency
101 W. James St.
(717) 394-0770

Preferred Travel and Incentives
229 N. Concord St.
(717) 399-7992

Zeller Travel
27 W. Lemon St.
(717) 299-8943

Students Speak Out On...
Transcription

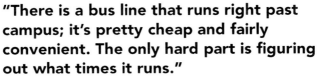

"There is a bus line that runs right past campus; it's pretty cheap and fairly convenient. The only hard part is figuring out what times it runs."

Q "Red Rose Transit Authority is the bus service. It's free on Saturdays in the fall. But **it's best to walk or drive around**."

Q "It's **not convenient at all**. It helps to have a car or to have a friend who has one."

Q "Transportation is **extremely convenient**, plus almost everything is within walking distance."

Q "I've always had my car or a friend, so I never used public transportation, but there are maps, **or visit the college information center for bus schedules**."

Q "There is **not much in the way of public transportation**, but there is quite a bit within walking distance."

Q "There's public transportation in Lancaster? It's not convenient at all. **It's best to bring a car to school**, if at all possible. Otherwise, just make friends with people who do have cars—that is the best way to get around."

Q "**I walk everywhere**—movies, city—everywhere."

Q "**What public transportation**?"

The College Prowler Take On...
Transportation

RRTA has 18 bus routes. The most popular route, which goes both downtown and to the Park City Center, has a stop on campus across from Old Main. Schedules are distributed at the Information Desk in the Steinman College Center. The bus system is convenient and easy for those who grew up using the buses. For suburbanites and their attack SUVs, I'm afraid the situation is not quite so sanguine. If you're not willing to work a little to understand the buses, find a friend with a car and stick to them like glue!

Students use several local airports, including those in Philly, New York, and DC. Transportation is easiest to Philly or New York, with a great train connection at the downtown Philly station. Again, most students prefer to catch rides with friends to airports and the train station. If you're determined, you can get around, but Lancaster doesn't make it easy on you.

The College Prowler® Grade on

Transportation: D

A high grade for Transportation indicates that campus buses, public buses, cabs, and rental cars are readily-available and affordable. Other determining factors include proximity to an airport and the necessity of transportation.

Weather

The Lowdown On...
Weather

Average Temperature:

Fall:	56 °F
Winter:	29 °F
Spring:	50 °F
Summer:	73 °F

Average Precipitation:

Fall:	7.20 in.
Winter:	21.5 in.
Spring:	7.80 in.
Summer:	12.4 in.

Students Speak Out On...
Weather

"The weather is diverse. It will snow, hail, rain, and be 98 degrees, maybe even in the same month. Expect changes, and pack for both cold and hot weather."

Q "It gets very cold here in the winter, but **we do have seasons**—it's the Northeast."

Q "The weather is seasonal, so you will wear shorts and T-shirts when you come at the end of summer and in the spring-time. Jeans/sweatshirts for the fall, and a nice parka for the winter. It also rains a lot in Pennsylvania so **bring an umbrella if you don't want to get wet**. Lancaster isn't that swift with cleaning up wintertime slush, snow, and ice, and the campus is no exception. When the first snow falls, expect everyone to look around in horror, and then proceed to not clean it up. I'm bringing a pair of sturdy, waterproof boots next year to better brave the rain and snow. Sneakers just don't cut it in bad weather, unless you enjoy being damp. Never fear, though—springtime is beautiful, as there are lots of flowers and sunshine and outdoorsy activities. Yay!"

Q "The weather can be gross, especially since it rains a lot. It is **really hot when you first get here** and really cold in the winter. All parts of the spectrum are covered."

Q "In the summer, it's hot and humid at times, so bring shorts and a T-shirt. In the fall, jeans are good, and in the winter, sweaters. **In spring, you will be wearing T-shirts**, but it's usually rainy in March and April."

Q "There are **a few big snow storms each year**. Bring at least one really warm jacket."

Q "I've never given much thought to the weather because it's exactly like the weather at home for me (New Jersey). But there are four seasons, so bring clothing that is appropriate for each season. Also, **it rains a lot in Lancaster** for some reason, so bring an umbrella. It can get really cold in the winter, so a heavy winter jacket is good, too. Otherwise, just dress accordingly, I suppose."

Q "**Plan for a mix of cold winters and hot summers**, but really the weather's actually very pleasant!"

The College Prowler Take On...
Weather

Gorgeous days aren't unheard of, but really, really crummy days aren't, either. Saying that the weather varies widely is, if anything, an understatement. The past couple winters have had snowfalls that ranged from nine inches to 63 inches in all, although 20 to 30 is more typical. Of course, whenever it snows, Fummers make sleds out of dining hall trays and cavort down Buchanan Hill with the local children for fun!

There are a lot of really nice days in the spring and fall. And when that happens, F&M students take advantage of it by sitting out in the sunshine and playing Frisbee. The campus itself is gorgeous year-round, whatever the weather might be.

The College Prowler® Grade on

Weather: B-

A high Weather grade designates that temperatures are mild and rarely reach extremes, that the campus tends to be sunny rather than rainy, and that weather is fairly consistent rather than unpredictable.

Report Card Summary

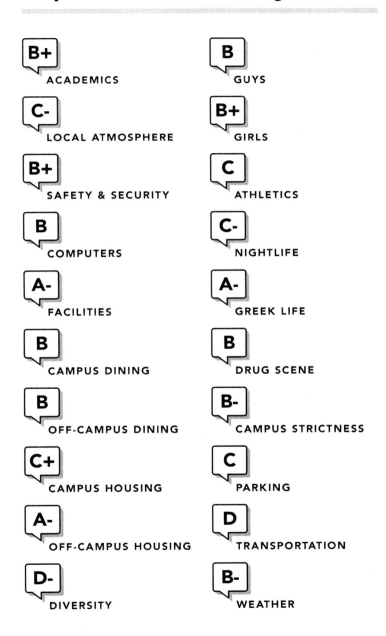

B+ ACADEMICS

C- LOCAL ATMOSPHERE

B+ SAFETY & SECURITY

B COMPUTERS

A- FACILITIES

B CAMPUS DINING

B OFF-CAMPUS DINING

C+ CAMPUS HOUSING

A- OFF-CAMPUS HOUSING

D- DIVERSITY

B GUYS

B+ GIRLS

C ATHLETICS

C- NIGHTLIFE

A- GREEK LIFE

B DRUG SCENE

B- CAMPUS STRICTNESS

C PARKING

D TRANSPORTATION

B- WEATHER

Overall Experience

Students Speak Out On...
Overall Experience

{ **"I can picture myself nowhere else. I am a member of a wonderful community. I feel safe, inspired, and enriched—it's a great place!"**

Q "It's hard to say what other places would have been like. **I am just finding my place now** at the end of my second year. But, if I could change things, I wouldn't have come here."

Q "So far, my experience has been amazing. Through my activities, I have found **some of the most wonderful people ever**, and I feel I have grown a lot as a person."

Q "**I've loved my experience at F&M**. I've made great friends, I've learned a lot from my professors in and outside the classroom, and had many great opportunities. I wouldn't trade my college for the world."

Q "**I love it here**."

Q "I'm so glad I chose F&M. **It has allowed me to grow** intellectually and personally."

Q "I absolutely love F&M. My overall experience has been just fantastic. I have never been or felt so happy in all my life, and I've never been able to fit in or succeed so well before. **I have great friends at F&M** and amazing sorority sisters, and I don't think that I would have been this happy at any other college I applied to. And to be honest, I hear this from most people. F&M is a great college community and I'm happy to be a part of it."

Q "**I love it here**! I wouldn't be a tour guide here in the middle of the summer if I didn't love it!"

Q "I'm staying at F&M forever! **I can't imagine being anywhere else**, and I'm counting down the moments until I can go back."

Q "I enjoyed being in college and F&M itself was okay. **I do wish that I was somewhere more liberal**. I feel that the students and faculty here are not as open-minded as the school portrays them to be."

The College Prowler Take On...
Overall Experience

However much they may complain, Fummers love it here. Once they've found their niche, they're the happiest little bunch of workaholics you'll ever meet. The only regrets come from those people who expected college to be a series of protests and consciousness-raising. You can have those experiences if you really want to, but in all probability, you'll have to organize them.

The most usual F&M experience follows a pattern: as you come to know the school, you get to know people, and your initial high hopes are met with reality. After a brief stint of disillusionment and dissatisfaction (this bit is optional), you'll come to recognize the wonders of F&M and meet the people whom you will hopefully stay close with, and you'll close out your experience having grown both academically and socially. Not a bad job for your four years!

The Inside Scoop

The Lowdown On...
The Inside Scoop

F&M Slang:

Know the slang, know the school. The following is a list of things you really need to know before coming to F&M. The more of these words you know, the better off you'll be.

A**F*** – The student nickname for the Alumni Sports and Fitness Center, derived from its acronym: ASFC. "I'm going over to the A**F***, want to come?"

Cake – Easy, as in a piece of. "Of course I don't mind putting a volunteer schedule together; it should be cake!"

CG – The Common Ground

Dip – An F&M student, short for Diplomat. F&M students appear to use this term unselfconsciously and non-ironically.

First-year student – A freshman anywhere else, but in gender-neutral terms.

Fry-daddy – A nickname for President John Fry. "Did you go see the Fry-daddy yesterday?"

FSA – The acronym for faculty, staff, and administration, this is a term that applies to just about everyone over the age of 23 on campus. Don't take their parking spots; they bite when provoked.

Fummer – An F&M student, which is not generally used in conversation; students prefer "dip" to "fummer."

The Green – The grassy space bounded by the infirmary, Dietz Hall, Steinman, and Schnader residence halls.

Hallcest – The unwise act of dating a person who lives on your residence hall. Very much discouraged for the sake of harmonious living!

I heart [blank] – Based off the pictorial representation of "I love," this is a gushing expression of affection. "Omigod, I heart F&M!"

OA – An orientation advisor, high-energy, upperclassmen volunteer to show first-years around. Their stock of ice-breaking games is legendary.

The Pit – Otherwise known as the Strength Training Center, which is a bastion of masculinity, you find yourself de-evolving the longer you spend time in this weight-lifting facility.

The Quad – The grassy space bounded by the Bens, Weis, Marshall-Buch, and Schnader residence halls.

RA – A resident assistant. Think of him or her as a stern older sibling, they'll help you out and advise you, but it's their job to bust you when you act stupid. Keep your hall clean and quiet and they'll love you for it.

Sexile – The act of relegating one's roommate from the bedroom in order to engage in sexual activities.

Shaddy/Shad-Fack – Nickname for the social science and humanities library, really named Shadek-Fackenthal Library.

Things I Wish I Knew Before Coming to F&M

- F&M students like to have snowball fights at the first signs of snow, so remember boots, gloves, and a snow jacket.

- Grades don't matter—no, really. All that matters is what you learn (as long as you pass). Nobody really cares what your GPA was.

- The professors really want you to succeed. They'll bend over backwards for you if you show a little initiative.

Tips to Succeed at F&M

- Participate in Orientation. It's your last chance for the really, really dumb questions.

- But don't go to Dave Binder's show—trust me.

- Go to class. Really. Get to know your professors. Go visit them in their offices—they get lonely.

- Get a really good planner and learn to manage your time.

- Get a support system: join a club, a church group, or Greek organization.

- Get involved! Do something you never would have thought you'd like. Be open to new people and new experiences. But don't join so much that you don't have time to do your schoolwork!

- Do a preceptorship or research project and use all of F&M's resources.

- Avoid the library—get your research done and get out. It's a roach motel: easy to get into, impossible to leave. They also crank the heat—you'll fall asleep over your books.

F&M Urban Legends

- Old Main, the building that houses administrative offices and the president's office, was built on the highest hill in the area. It was also built at the site of the gibbet—the hanging tree. Many restless spirits have been witnessed late at night, and sometimes, the bells of Old Main ring in the middle of the night.

- The two buildings that abut Old Main, Diagnothian and Goethian Halls, were used as Union hospitals during the Civil War. Allegedly, if music is played that mentions war in either building, clanking and moaning can be clearly heard throughout the building.

- Shadek-Fackenthal Library hosts a number of scholars—one of whom is deceased. The northeast study room on the third floor hosts Dr. Harvey Bassler, who died tragically in 1950. Students closing up the library frequently find books on the Pennsylvania Dutch strewn about his old workspace, and strange noises are reported from the floor below at 10 p.m. on the nose, Dr. Bassler's time of death.

- Wohlsen House, the admission building, boasts a number of strange occurrences—door slamming, flickering lights, and odd noises. The oddest of these occurrences is the most entertaining. With some regularity, if people are there late at night, all of the lights go out at once, but if someone remembers to shout, "Cut it out, Bob!" or "Knock it off, Bob," the lights are immediately restored.

- Wohlsen House was also a fraternity house for Lambda Chi Alpha until the school reclaimed it in 1982. It is rumored that upon its repossession, several fraternity brothers drove a car through its front window in retaliation. This story can neither be confirmed nor denied, as Lambda Chi no longer exists at F&M which in itself is telling.

- Stager Hall's most famous story is of the senseless murder of Marion Baker in 1950. Ms. Baker, an employee of the college in then Stahr Hall, was only 21 when she ran into Edward Gibbs, a 25-year-old F&M senior and WWII veteran. He offered her a ride to campus after an errand, but he drove her to a remote area and bludgeoned her to death instead. He turned himself into President Distler a few days later, with no explanation for his actions other than "impulse." He was sentenced to death and was executed in the electric chair in 1951.

- The squirrels are ready to take over the school. They have trained an elite force to leap out at unsuspecting students from the trash bins along the Quad and Green, attack them, and steal their take-away French fries from the CG. In all seriousness, the squirrels are huge and scary and prone to leaping at the unwary from trees. Watch your food—and your head.

School Spirit

Students kick off their years here with Orientation. Their OAs (Orientation Advisors: one or two per hall) and RAs (one per hall) try to instill hall spirit right away. By the Pajama Parade, most first-years are chanting their hall with the best of them, and that loyalty typically lasts for the duration.

Dips also get rallied for basketball games, but few other sports. Rugby games are always good for a few screams, and of course we rally around the winning teams (of which there's usually at least one a season). But don't expect a frenzy like at a state school—Dips are still more concerned for their studies than for sports teams.

Of course, we'll wear F&M gear until the cows come home (never an idle threat in Amish country), and that's good enough for most of us.

Traditions

Ben-in-the-Box

A less savory tradition is one revolving around the statue of Ben-in-the-box next to Keiper Hall. Late at night, young men (and certain among the more adventurous young women) urinate at his base as an initiation rite of sorts. Whatever you do, don't touch the statue!

Create Your Own

F&M's traditions tend to be more spur-of-the-moment, generally. We have very little compunction about making them up as we go, and few of us feel guilty about that. We have so much history, you see, that everything balances out. If you want to start one, go for it!

Flapjack Fest

Every Reading Weekend, the day before finals begin, the Flapjack Fest takes place. FSA serves breakfast to fidgety scholars from 9 p.m. to midnight, teasing them about their upcoming exams. This is a wonderful time to relax, spend time with your friends, and frantically exchange chemistry notes with your lab partner—just kidding!

Fum Follies

In a similar vein, every few years, the faculty, staff, and administration get together under the guidance of talented musicians and librettists, and perform Fum Follies, a revue parodying some aspect of student life, college history, and current events.

Pajama Parade

All first-year students, as a part of First-Year Orientation, participate in the pajama parade. As halls, they decorate banners, perform skits, and choreograph dance routines. These skits have typically demonstrated great hall spirit (Mighty Mighty Second Dubbs), as well as some aspect of college history. The merging of the colleges, the decision to go coed, or the schools' original founding are all fair game.

Traying

The trays from the dining hall make great sleds, and there are more than a few quality hills in Buchanan Park. Steal one the first time it snows and sled your heart out! But remember to return the tray, or Dining Services gets cranky.

Finding a Job or Internship

The Lowdown On...
Finding a Job or Internship

Franklin & Marshall students are in high demand with those who know what they're getting. Squeeze every bit of use out of Career Services that you can get, but you'll have to have plenty of get-up-and-go to score the hottest jobs and internships.

Advice

Network, network, network. Tell everyone you know that you're looking for a job or internship, and chances are they'll know someone who does. If all else fails, go to the Jobs Database (*www.fandm.edu/departments/financialaid/ bb*) and check out the postings, both on and off campus.

Career Center Resources & Services

Career Advisement Services
701 College Ave.

(717) 291-4084

Alumni directory, business dress, cover letters, electronic recruiting databases, interviewing, membership in the selective liberal arts consortium for seniors and recent grads, table manners, test preparation courses, workshops on resumes

Firms that Most Frequently Hire Graduates

Chubb Insurance, Ernst and Young, JP Morgan, Merrill Lynch

Alumni

The Lowdown On...
Alumni

Web Site:
http://alumni.fandm.edu

Services Available:
Free lifetime e-mail
Online network

Alumni Office:
Alumni On-Line
Franklin & Marshall College
P.O. Box 3003
Lancaster, PA 17604-3003

(717) 291-3973

Major Alumni Events

Alumni Weekend is the major event for the year, which includes class reunions, scholar breakfasts, and a number of Greek events. Other events, such as get-togethers, are scheduled through the online alumni network.

Alumni Publication

The *Franklin and Marshall Magazine* is published quarterly by the Office of College Communications, featuring campus news and special accomplishments.

Did You Know?

Famous F&M Alumni:

James Lapine – Playwright

Franklin Schaffner – Director

Roy Scheider – Actor

Glen Tetley – Choreographer

Treat Williams – Actor

Student Organizations

The following is a sampling of F&M's student organizations. For the most up-to-date list, check out *www.fandm.edu/clubs.xml*, or contact the Office of Student Activities.

Acting Up!
African Club
African Dance Troupe
African Drumming Club
African Student Union
Aikido
American Chemical Society
Amnesty International
Anime
Anthropology Club
Asian Cultural Society
Badminton Club
Ben's Underground

Black Pyramid
Black Student Union
Cheerleading
Chessmen
Ciao Bella
College Democrats
College Dispatch
College Entertainment Committee
College Republicans
Crew
Dance Club
Dance Team

Dance Revolution Club

Eastern European Club

Environmental
Action Alliance

F&M C.A.R.E.S.

F&M Players

Free Culture Society

Gaming Society

Geological Society

German Club

Gourmet Society

Government Club

Habitat for Humanity

Hillel

Ice Hockey

IMPACT

International Club

Intervarsity Christian
Fellowship

John Newman Association

LGBTA

Mi Genta Latina

Mu Upsilon Sigma

Nur-al-Islam

Oriflamme

Oxfam

Philosophy Club

Physics Club

Plume

Poor Richards

Porter Scientific Society

Pre-Dental Club

Pre-Vet Club

Prolog

SAVE

SETA

SISTERS

Spanish Club

Spring Arts Council

Student Alumni Association

Students Committed
to Social Change

Students for
Marriage Equality

Sweet Ophelia

Swing and Ballroom

Traditions Committee

Ultimate Frisbee

Voices of Praise

VOX

WFNM

Women's Center

The Best
& Worst

The Ten BEST Things About F&M

1	Cricket matches on the Green in nice weather
2	Frisbee matches on the Quad in nice weather
3	The professors
4	Precepting
5	The wireless network
6	Coed halls
7	The ASFC
8	Spring Arts Weekend
9	Roschel Performing Arts Center
10	Flapjack Fest

The Ten **WORST** Things About F&M

1 The football team

2 The mascot

3 Attacking squirrels

4 Complaining students

5 Rising student apathy

6 Coed bathrooms

7 The Pit

8 Finals week

9 The distance from New York City

10 The smell when we're downwind from the farms

Visiting

The Lowdown On...
Visiting

Hotel Information:
Check with hotels for discounts to F&M visitors.

Apple Bin Inn (Bed & Breakfast)
2835 Willow St. Pike
(717) 464-5881
www.applebininn.com
Distance from Campus: 4.4 miles
Price Range: $115–$175

Best Western Eden Resort Inn
222 Eden Rd.
(717) 569-6444
www.edenresort.com
Distance from Campus: 2.8 miles
Price Range: $100–$170

→

Comfort Inn
50 Centerville Rd.
(717) 898-2431
www.choicehotels.com
Distance from Campus:
5.8 miles
Price Range: $85–$105

Hampton Inn
545 Greenfield Rd
(717) 299-1200
http://hamptoninn.com
Distance from Campus:
4.9 miles
Price Range: $94–$114

Hilton Garden Inn
101 Granite Run Dr.
(717) 560-0880
www.hilton.com
Distance from campus:
2.8 miles
Price Range: $90–$110

Holiday Inn East
521 Greenfield Rd.
(717) 299-2551
www.holiday-inn.com
Distance from Campus:
4.9 miles
Price Range: $70–$90

**King's Cottage
(Bed & Breakfast)**
1049 E. King St.
(717) 397-1017
www.kingscottagebb.com
Distance from campus:
2.6 miles
Price Range: $165–$270

Take a Campus Virtual Tour

http://admission.fandm.edu/tour

To Schedule a Group Information Session or Interview

Call Admissions to set up an interview at (877) 678-9111 or go to the Web site for further details at *http://admission. fandm.edu/visit*. Individual interviews or information sessions with an admission counselor must be pre-arranged, but no reservations have to be made for campus tours.

Campus Tours

Tours are offered throughout the year Monday through Friday at 10 a.m., 11 a.m., 2 p.m., and 3 p.m. No appointment is necessary, but call if you plan to be there during a holiday or semester break.

Overnight Visits

Highly recommended! You can request an overnight visit by calling admissions at (877) 678-9111.

Directions to Campus

Driving from the North

From Northeastern Pennsylvania/Upstate New York

- Follow Route 81 South and take exit 30 (Route 72 South).
- Follow Route 72 South to Lancaster area.
- Approximately 2-3 miles from the Route 30/Route 72 junction, turn right at traffic light onto Dillerville Road.
- At next light, turn left onto Harrisburg Pike Franklin & Marshall is 0.5 mile ahead on your right.

From New Jersey/Eastern New York/New England

- Take the New Jersey Turnpike to exit 6 (Pennsylvania Turnpike west).
- Take the PA Turnpike west to exit 21 (Lancaster/Reading/Route 222 South).
- Take Route 222 South approximately 14 miles to the Lancaster area.
- Stay to the right and follow signs for Route 30 west (York).
- Pass Oregon, Lititz and Fruitville Pikes. Just beyond Fruitville Pike, exit to continue on 30 west (York).
- Take first exit for Harrisburg Pike (The Park City Center will be on right).
- At the top of the exit ramp, turn left onto Harrisburg Pike.
- Proceed 1.5 miles through several traffic lights toward Franklin & Marshall and follow signs for Office of Admission parking.

Driving from the South

From Baltimore/Washington and South

- From Baltimore Beltway (Route 695), exit onto Route 83 North.
- Follow Route 83 North to York, PA.
- Take exit 9E (Arsenal Road/Route 30 east).
- Take Route 30 east to Lancaster (approximately 20 miles).
- Take the exit for Harrisburg Pike.
- Turn right at the light at the top of the exit ramp and proceed toward Lancaster City.
- Franklin & Marshall is about 1.5 miles and several traffic lights ahead on your right. Follow signs for Office of Admission parking.

From Delaware

- Follow Route 41 North from Hockessin, DE to Route 30 junction in Gap, PA.
- Turn left at the light at the 41/30 junction onto Route 30 west toward Lancaster.
- Follow Route 30 West for approximately 20 minutes. You will pass the shopping outlets and continue to follow 30 west until it becomes a 2 lane highway.
- Pass Oregon, Lititz and Fruitville Pikes. Just beyond Fruitville Pike, exit to continue on 30 West (York).
- Take first exit for Harrisburg Pike (The Park City Center will be on right).
- At the top of the exit ramp, turn left onto Harrisburg Pike.
- Proceed 1.5 miles through several traffic lights toward Franklin & Marshall and follow signs for Office of Admission parking.

Driving from the East

From Philadelphia

- Take the Pennsylvania Turnpike west to exit 21 (Lancaster/Reading/Route 222 South).
- Follow Route 222 South approximately 14 miles to the Lancaster area.
- Stay to the right and follow signs for Route 30 West (York).
- Pass Oregon, Lititz and Fruitville Pikes. Just beyond Fruitville Pike, exit to continue on 30 West (York).
- Take first exit for Harrisburg Pike (The Park City Center will be on right).
- At the top of the exit ramp, turn left onto Harrisburg Pike.
- Proceed 1.5 miles through several traffic lights toward Franklin & Marshall and follow signs for Office of Admission parking.

Driving from the West

From Harrisburg and Central Pennsylvania

- From north of Harrisburg, take Route 15 South to Route 322 East.
- Cross the Susquehanna River and follow to Routes 81 North/322 East.
- From Routes 81 North/322 East, take Route 83 south to Route 283 South.
- From Route 283 South, exit onto Route 283 East (Lancaster).
- Take Route 283 East to Route 30 West towards York.
- Take the first exit for Harrisburg Pike (The Park City Center will be on right).
- At the top of the exit ramp, turn left onto Harrisburg Pike
- Proceed 1.5 miles through several traffic lights toward Franklin & Marshall and follow signs for Office of Admission parking.

From Western Pennsylvania

- Take Pennsylvania Turnpike to Exit 19 (Harrisburg East).
- Take first exit to your right immediately out of tollbooth to get onto Route 283 East.
- Take Route 283 East to Route 30 West towards York.
- Take the first exit for Harrisburg Pike (The Park City Center will be on right).
- At the top of the exit ramp, turn left onto Harrisburg Pike.
- Proceed 1.5 miles through several traffic lights toward Franklin & Marshall and follow signs for Office of Admission parking.

Words to Know

Academic Probation – A suspension imposed on a student if he or she fails to keep up with the school's minimum academic requirements. Those unable to improve their grades after receiving this warning can face dismissal.

Beer Pong/Beirut – A drinking game involving cups of beer arranged in a pyramid shape on each side of a table. The goal is to get a ping pong ball into one of the opponent's cups by throwing the ball or hitting it with a paddle. If the ball lands in a cup, the opponent is required to drink the beer.

Bid – An invitation from a fraternity or sorority to 'pledge' (join) that specific house.

Blue-Light Phone – Brightly-colored phone posts with a blue light bulb on top. These phones exist for security purposes and are located at various outside locations around most campuses. In an emergency, a student can pick up one of these phones (free of charge) to connect with campus police or a security escort.

Campus Police – Police who are specifically assigned to a given institution. Campus police are typically not regular city officers; they are employed by the university in a full-time capacity.

Club Sports – A level of sports that falls somewhere between varsity and intramural. If a student is unable to commit to a varsity team but has a lot of passion for athletics, a club sport could be a better, less intense option. Even less demanding, intramural (IM) sports often involve no traveling and considerably less time.

Cocaine – An illegal drug. Also known as "coke" or "blow," cocaine often resembles a white crystalline or powdery substance. It is highly addictive and dangerous.

Common Application – An application with which students can apply to multiple schools.

Course Registration – The period of official class selection for the upcoming quarter or semester. Prior to registration, it is best to prepare several back-up courses in case a particular class becomes full. If a course is full, students can place themselves on the waitlist, although this still does not guarantee entry.

Division Athletics – Athletic classifications range from Division I to Division III. Division IA is the most competitive, while Division III is considered to be the least competitive.

Dorm – A dorm (or dormitory) is an on-campus housing facility. Dorms can provide a range of options from suite-style rooms to more communal options that include shared bathrooms. Most first-year students live in dorms. Some upperclassmen who wish to stay on campus also choose this option.

Early Action – An application option with which a student can apply to a school and receive an early acceptance response without a binding commitment. This system is becoming less and less available.

Early Decision – An application option that students should use only if they are certain they plan to attend the school in question. If a student applies using the early decision option and is admitted, he or she is required and bound to attend that university. Admission rates are usually higher among students who apply through early decision, as the student is clearly indicating that the school is his or her first choice.

Ecstasy – An illegal drug. Also known as "E" or "X," ecstasy looks like a pill and most resembles an aspirin. Considered a party drug, ecstasy is very dangerous and can be deadly.

Ethernet – An extremely fast Internet connection available in most university-owned residence halls. To use an Ethernet connection properly, a student will need a network card and cable for his or her computer.

Fake ID – A counterfeit identification card that contains false information. Most commonly, students get fake IDs with altered birthdates so that they appear to be older than 21 (and therefore of legal drinking age). Even though it is illegal, many college students have fake IDs in hopes of purchasing alcohol or getting into bars.

Frosh – Slang for "freshman" or "freshmen."

Hazing – Initiation rituals administered by some fraternities or sororities as part of the pledging process. Many universities have outlawed hazing due to its degrading, and sometimes dangerous, nature.

Intramurals (IMs) – A popular, and usually free, sport league in which students create teams and compete against one another. These sports vary in competitiveness and can include a range of activities—everything from billiards to water polo. IM sports are a great way to meet people with similar interests.

Keg – Officially called a half-barrel, a keg contains roughly 200 12-ounce servings of beer.

LSD – An illegal drug, also known as acid, this hallucinogenic drug most commonly resembles a tab of paper.

Marijuana – An illegal drug, also known as weed or pot; along with alcohol, marijuana is one of the most commonly-found drugs on campuses across the country.

Major –The focal point of a student's college studies; a specific topic that is studied for a degree. Examples of majors include physics, English, history, computer science, economics, business, and music. Many students decide on a specific major before arriving on campus, while others are simply "undecided" until declaring a major. Those who are extremely interested in two areas can also choose to double major.

Meal Block – The equivalent of one meal. Students on a meal plan usually receive a fixed number of meals per week. Each meal, or "block," can be redeemed at the school's dining facilities in place of cash. Often, a student's weekly allotment of meal blocks will be forfeited if not used.

Minor – An additional focal point in a student's education. Often serving as a complement or addition to a student's main area of focus, a minor has fewer requirements and prerequisites to fulfill than a major. Minors are not required for graduation from most schools; however some students who want to explore many different interests choose to pursue both a major and a minor.

Mushrooms – An illegal drug. Also known as "'shrooms," this drug resembles regular mushrooms but is extremely hallucinogenic.

Off-Campus Housing – Housing from a particular landlord or rental group that is not affiliated with the university. Depending on the college, off-campus housing can range from extremely popular to non-existent. Students who choose to live off campus are typically given more freedom, but they also have to deal with possible subletting scenarios, furniture, bills, and other issues. In addition to these factors, rental prices and distance often affect a student's decision to move off campus.

Office Hours – Time that teachers set aside for students who have questions about coursework. Office hours are a good forum for students to go over any problems and to show interest in the subject material.

Pledging – The early phase of joining a fraternity or sorority, pledging takes place after a student has gone through rush and received a bid. Pledging usually lasts between one and two semesters. Once the pledging period is complete and a particular student has done everything that is required to become a member, that student is considered a brother or sister. If a fraternity or a sorority would decide to "haze" a group of students, this initiation would take place during the pledging period.

Private Institution – A school that does not use tax revenue to subsidize education costs. Private schools typically cost more than public schools and are usually smaller.

Prof – Slang for "professor."

Public Institution – A school that uses tax revenue to subsidize education costs. Public schools are often a good value for in-state residents and tend to be larger than most private colleges.

Quarter System (or Trimester System) – A type of academic calendar system. In this setup, students take classes for three academic periods. The first quarter usually starts in late September or early October and concludes right before Christmas. The second quarter usually starts around early to mid–January and finishes up around March or April. The last academic quarter, or "third quarter," usually starts in late March or early April and finishes up in late May or Mid-June. The fourth quarter is summer. The major difference between the quarter system and semester system is that students take more, less comprehensive courses under the quarter calendar.

RA (Resident Assistant) – A student leader who is assigned to a particular floor in a dormitory in order to help to the other students who live there. An RA's duties include ensuring student safety and providing assistance wherever possible.

Recitation – An extension of a specific course; a review session. Some classes, particularly large lectures, are supplemented with mandatory recitation sessions that provide a relatively personal class setting.

Rolling Admissions – A form of admissions. Most commonly found at public institutions, schools with this type of policy continue to accept students throughout the year until their class sizes are met. For example, some schools begin accepting students as early as December and will continue to do so until April or May.

Room and Board – This figure is typically the combined cost of a university-owned room and a meal plan.

Room Draw/Housing Lottery – A common way to pick on-campus room assignments for the following year. If a student decides to remain in university-owned housing, he or she is assigned a unique number that, along with seniority, is used to determine his or her housing for the next year.

Rush – The period in which students can meet the brothers and sisters of a particular chapter and find out if a given fraternity or sorority is right for them. Rushing a fraternity or a sorority is not a requirement at any school. The goal of rush is to give students who are serious about pledging a feel for what to expect.

Semester System – The most common type of academic calendar system at college campuses. This setup typically includes two semesters in a given school year. The fall semester starts around the end of August or early September and concludes before winter vacation. The spring semester usually starts in mid-January and ends in late April or May.

Student Center/Rec Center/Student Union – A common area on campus that often contains study areas, recreation facilities, and eateries. This building is often a good place to meet up with fellow students; depending on the school, the student center can have a huge role or a non-existent role in campus life.

Student ID – A university-issued photo ID that serves as a student's key to school-related functions. Some schools require students to show these cards in order to get into dorms, libraries, cafeterias, and other facilities. In addition to storing meal plan information, in some cases, a student ID can actually work as a debit card and allow students to purchase things from bookstores or local shops.

Suite – A type of dorm room. Unlike dorms that feature communal bathrooms shared by the entire floor, suites offer bathrooms shared only among the suite. Suite-style dorm rooms can house anywhere from two to ten students.

TA (Teacher's Assistant) – An undergraduate or grad student who helps in some manner with a specific course. In some cases, a TA will teach a class, assist a professor, grade assignments, or conduct office hours.

Undergraduate – A student in the process of studying for his or her bachelor's degree.

ABOUT THE AUTHOR

I am a graduate of Franklin & Marshall College, where I was honored to be the 83rd recipient of the Henry S. Williamson Medal. Right now, I live and work in Burlington, Vermont, but I originally hail from Collinsville, Illinois.

I would also like to take this opportunity to thank my loving sisters Robyn, Sara, Megs, Shahed, and Marisa for their help and support with this project, as well as my friends Sarah, Obs, Amy, Kristen, Jamie, Lea, and Jess. I love you guys!

Ellen Baier
ellenbaier@collegeprowler.com

Notes

....

....

....

....

....

....

....

....

....

....

....

....

....

Notes

....

....

....

....

....

....

....

....

....

....

....

....

....

Notes

....

....

....

....

....

....

....

....

....

....

....

....

....

Notes

Notes

....

....

....

....

....

....

....

....

....

....

....

....

....

Notes

....

....

....

....

....

....

....

....

....

....

....

....

....

Notes

....

....

....

....

....

....

....

....

....

....

....

....

....

Notes

....

....

....

....

....

....

....

....

....

....

....

....

....

Notes

....

....

....

....

....

....

....

....

....

....

....

....

....

Notes

....

....

....

....

....

....

....

....

....

....

....

....

....

Notes

....

....

....

....

....

....

....

....

....

....

....

....

....

Notes

....

....

....

....

....

....

....

....

....

....

....

....

....

Notes

....
....
....
....
....
....
....
....
....
....
....
....
....

Notes

Notes

....

....

....

....

....

....

....

....

....

....

....

....

....

Notes

....

....

....

....

....

....

....

....

....

....

....

....

....

Notes

....

....

....

....

....

....

....

....

....

....

....

....

....

Notes

....
....
....
....
....
....
....
....
....
....
....
....
....

Notes

....

....

....

....

....

....

....

....

....

....

....

....

....

Notes

....

....

....

....

....

....

....

....

....

....

....

....

....

Notes

....

....

....

....

....

....

....

....

....

....

....

....

....

Notes

California Colleges

California dreamin'?

This book is a must have for you!

CALIFORNIA COLLEGES
7¼" X 10", 762 Pages Paperback
$29.95 Retail
1-59658-501-3

Stanford, UC Berkeley, Caltech—California is home
to some of America's greatest institutes of higher
learning. *California Colleges* gives the lowdown on 24
of the best, side by side, in one prodigious volume.

New England Colleges

Looking for peace in the Northeast?
Pick up this regional guide to New England!

NEW ENGLAND COLLEGES
7¼" X 10", 1015 Pages Paperback
$29.95 Retail
1-59658-504-8

New England is the birthplace of many prestigious universities, and with so many to choose from, picking the right school can be a tough decision. With inside information on over 34 competive Northeastern schools, *New England Colleges* provides the same high-quality information prospective students expect from College Prowler in one all-inclusive, easy-to-use reference.

Schools of the South

**Headin' down south? This book will help you
find your way to the perfect school!**

SCHOOLS OF THE SOUTH
7¼" X 10", 773 Pages Paperback
$29.95 Retail
1-59658-503-X

Southern pride is always strong. Whether it's across
town or across state, many Southern students are
devoted to their home sweet home. *Schools of the
South* offers an honest student perspective on 36
universities available south of the Mason-Dixon.

Untangling
the Ivy League

The ultimate book for everything Ivy!

UNTANGLING THE IVY LEAGUE
7¼" X 10", 567 Pages Paperback
$24.95 Retail
1-59658-500-5

Ivy League students, alumni, admissions officers,
and other top insiders get together to tell it like it is.
Untangling the Ivy League covers every aspect—from
admissions and athletics to secret societies and urban
legends—of the nation's eight oldest, wealthiest, and
most competitive colleges and universities.

Tell Us What Life Is Really Like at Your School!

Have you ever wanted to let people know what your college is really like? Now's your chance to help millions of high school students choose the right college.

Let your voice be heard.

Check out **www.collegeprowler.com** for more info!

Need More Help?

Do you have more questions about this school? Can't find a certain statistic? College Prowler is here to help. We are the best source of college information out there. We have a network of thousands of students who can get the latest information on any school to you ASAP. E-mail us at info@collegeprowler.com with your college-related questions.

E-Mail Us Your College-Related Questions!

Check out *www.collegeprowler.com* for more details.
1-800-290-2682

Write For Us!
Get published! Voice your opinion.

Writing a College Prowler guidebook is both fun and rewarding; our open-ended format allows your own creativity free reign. Our writers have been featured in national newspapers and have seen their names in bookstores across the country. Now is your chance to break into the publishing industry with one of the country's fastest-growing publishers!

Apply now at ***www.collegeprowler.com***

Contact editor@collegeprowler.com or call 1-800-290-2682 for more details.

Pros and Cons

Still can't figure out if this is the right school for you?
You've already read through this in-depth guide; why not
list the pros and cons? It will really help with narrowing down
your decision and determining whether or not
this school is right for you.

Pros	Cons
....	....
....	....
....	....
....	....
....	....
....	....
....	....
....	....
....	....
....	....
....	....
....	....
....	....

Pros and Cons

Still can't figure out if this is the right school for you?
You've already read through this in-depth guide; why not
list the pros and cons? It will really help with narrowing down
your decision and determining whether or not
this school is right for you.

Pros	Cons
....	....
....	....
....	....
....	....
....	....
....	....
....	....
....	....
....	....
....	....
....	....
....	....
....	....

Notes

To Brandon
From Mom and Dad

....
....
....
....
....
....
....
....
....
....
....
....
....
....

Notes

....

....

....

....

....

....

....

....

....

....

....

....

....